ON TELEVISION!

ON TELEVISION!

A SURVIVAL GUIDE
FOR MEDIA INTERVIEWS

JACK HILTON
MARY KNOBLAUCH

amacom

A Division of American Management Associations

Library of Congress Cataloging in Publication Data

Hilton, Jack, 1937-
    On television!

    Includes index.
    1. Interviewing in television. 2. Talk shows.
I. Knoblauch, Mary, joint author. II. Title.
PN1992.8.I68H5   791.45'5   80-65879
ISBN 0-8144-5627-8

First Printing

FOREWORD

Robert MacNeil

In 1968, after years of interviewing people on television myself, I learned what it was like to *be* interviewed. It was quite a revelation.

I appeared on a truncated version of the radio/television talk-show circuit to promote a book about television I had just published, called *The People Machine*. It never occurred to me that someone as experienced as I was at asking questions on television would find it so hard to answer them. But I did.

It was very difficult to dredge up from all I knew just the right material to respond to a question; to be sensational enough to tickle someone's curiosity, yet not distort or overstate the case for effect.

Even more difficult for me was the required compression. I am a very wordy fellow once I get going, a natural essay-type answerer. My wife says that if you ask me a question, you are likely to get a speech or a lecture in reply. I am also sensitive to qualifiers. I hate saying: this is so and that is not so, because I can often see many reasons why each may be partly so. Television does not love qualification. It hates the subjunctive voice. It was hell trying to squeeze all my wonderful thoughts into tough 100-word bursts with no equivocation. I was just getting warmed up when I could see the host's eyes begin to glaze over.

Even more frustrating was the knowledge that there on the pages of my book, lying virginal in the lap of the host, was everything I wanted to say, the thoughts neatly phrased, the facts logically marshaled. I kept thinking: if only I could remember just how I said it in the book.

The questions themselves also threw me. They always seemed to come from a different part of the forest from where my thoughts were. Some were very ignorant questions and some well informed. Some were mildly malicious and testing; most were well intentioned, even generous. But something put me off balance almost every time. The most upsetting questions were the extremely simple ones, like this, for instance: "What is wrong with TV news?" If you have just spent a year researching and writing a book on that topic, you don't know quite where to begin. You are tempted to throw out a terse, witty put-down (the kind that comes to mind while going to sleep that night) or to deliver an encyclopedic monologue.

Finally, what I found very disconcerting was the indifference in the eyes of the interviewers. Most of them managed to be professionally curious—they *looked* curious—but when I looked into their eyes, they weren't there. They were distracted.

It was on the *Mike Douglas Show* that I learned the secret truth: being interviewed is a lot easier than interviewing. If you know what you are talking about—and if it isn't something you have reason to be ashamed of—it is not a difficult experience. It's far easier, say, than standing up and making a speech.

Following instructions from the publisher's public relations people, I went early to Philadelphia where the *Mike Douglas Show* was taped and met the producer. He was a pleasant, somewhat distracted man, who was clearly going to be able to carry on living without knowing what I had to say to the world. He exuded an air which suggested that if they didn't have boring guests like me cluttering things up, they would have a far better show, and his wife and children would love him more.

Anyway, he got interested enough to ask me: "What do you want him to ask you?"

"What do you mean?" I said.

"What questions do you want Mike to ask?"

"Well," I gulped, "anything at all. I don't care."

The producer sighed, as the proprietess in a house of prostitution might sigh when shy clients need to be pushed into saying what they really want. "You realize that he hasn't read the book."

Finally I began dictating questions to the producer. It went slowly because, very efficiently, he was writing them directly on big cue cards with a squeaky felt-tip pen.

The taping began. Mike Douglas turned out to be one of those charismatic show business fellows who enfold you in their charm and professionalism. He had a knack of looking at me with the greatest interest and absorption, until his eyes flicked over my shoulder to the cue card to read the next question. His eyes then clicked back to mine again as he carefully listened to the answer. He stayed awake, the audience applauded a few times, and two fellow guests, who had actually read my book, waxed enthusiastic about it. I had just begun to think that I would like to do this for a living when it was over.

I went away with one lesson firmly learned, and being interviewed on television has never bothered me since that day. The lesson is: Know what you want to say, and use whatever questions you are asked to say it—briefly, along the way, you can actually address the questions put to you or not, as you choose. You can flatter the host by saying things like "That's a really interesting question," or "Now, I think that's the nub of the whole thing." Just don't get so fixated by the questions you are asked that you forget to make your points, assuming you have some.

The other thing I gradually learned is that practice helps. Being interviewed once is terrible. The fifth time is a lot better.

This book, *On Television!* is a useful introduction to such lessons. Its authors see the television landscape more heavily strewn with mines than I do. I don't believe it is very common, as they suggest, to find ambitious assistants lurking in the lobbies of TV stations waiting to overhear some indiscretion and pass it on to the interviewer. I don't believe that news programs are as alert to what is said on talk shows as they suggest, or as eager to pick up excerpts, unless the guest is very newsworthy.

Some people might argue with the presumption that the television medium is the regular army, the

established power, which poor, powerless busi-
nessmen are forced to infiltrate and sabotage like
guerrillas. But I put some of that down to business
paranoia. In its central thrust, this book is right on
target. It is a good chart for navigating undeniably
tricky waters.

For their epigraph, the authors include a section
of the code of conduct of the National Association of
Broadcasters. It says: "interview/discussion programs . . . should be governed by acceptable
standards of ethical journalism." That is clearly an
acknowledgment that, at least in some such programs, acceptable journalistic standards are not
followed.

Television has become the mass journalism of our
day. Without doubt it will remain so, but its preemi-
nence will probably grow. Its journalistic output is not,
however, confined to programs that carry the label
"news." Publishing topical information or opinion *is*
journalism, and American television and radio stations do a lot of that under other headings. They may
think of such programs as entertainment, or public
service, or religious broadcasting, or consumer
information, but in the broadest sense it is all
journalism, and it is all subject to the same regulations as news programs, for example, the Fairness
Doctrine or the equal-time provision. (In fact, news
programs may be exempt from some regulations that
govern the rest.) Such "entertainment" programs are
also clearly governed by the laws against libel and
slander. In other words, the stations are as responsible for the content of non-news shows as they are for
the content of news programs. Yet very different
standards apply.

The talk-show host is far more a law unto himself

than the television newsman. He can be as eccentric as he likes in his choice of subjects. He can get by with no preparation and play it by ear, whatever the interview situation. He can argue with his guests, challenge their views, make jokes at their expense, air his own prejudices, and generally play God—no one will bat an eye. He is not even required to ask questions a journalist would consider relevant. He need never be burdened by mere facts. All he must follow is his own inner ear, his sense of what his audience will find interesting or amusing.

Such programs *may* be as responsible as TV news. Some may be a good deal more responsible, but often they are so freewheeling, so improvised, and even sometimes so irresponsible that it is not surprising for an inexperienced guest from the world of business or the professions to feel bewildered and defenseless. The frame of reference is vague: he doesn't know whether he is there to be laughed at, harangued, or applauded. Most of the advice in this book is intended to help guests on talk shows like these, and the advice is sensible.

My impression is, like the authors', that on such programs a guest is more likely to be deferred to and flattered than attacked.

It is on the local television news that a person interviewed needs to be wary. Few news interviews are done "live." Most are recorded on film or tape, taken back to the studio, and a "bite" selected from all that was shot to represent the interviewee's side of the story. That bite may be as brief as thirty seconds or as long as a few minutes, even though the camera crew and the reporter on the scene will have shot many times that amount. The bite that is selected may or may not represent the thrust of what the person interviewed intended to say. It may convey no glaring misrepresentation of his position yet leave a definite feeling that that wasn't how he intended to say it. It may have been a response drawn from him in answer to a question and yet presented in a way that suggests he volunteered the statement, a standard device of newspapers and wire services that makes people feel they have been quoted "out of context."

With television increasingly replacing newspapers as the source of competitive journalism in many cities, that cry is heard more often. Something about television makes the practice seem more egregious, because by its very nature, television is more credible. Surveys continue to show that more people get their news from television and find it more trustworthy than they do newspapers or magazines. Just to see and hear a man on television has some power to make you believe that what you see is what he said. Yet it may be only a small, and possibly prejudicial, part of what he said.

There are ways of coping with the danger: officers of corporations who are likely to be spokesmen on television when a news story breaks can school themselves in ways of keeping their message short and quotable as it stands. This book will help them do that. They can, if they wish, insist that their interview be run unedited. Many stations will balk, but some will go along.

Learning all the tricks is not a substitute for having a good case, and it is fatal to leave good press relations until a crisis forces the issue. Businesses would be wise to practice what politicians have done for years. They cultivate and befriend TV newsmen when there is no crisis. It is not a question of "buying" the journalist, but educating him in the concerns and the realities of whatever the business is. When there is a crisis, or a hot news story, that newsman will at the very least be more receptive to your point of view.

In fact, I don't share the widespread impression that television is out stalking business executives to make fools of them. Television newsmen line their studies with congratulatory plaques from business associations, not the scalps of company officers.

It is fashionable in television to apply the investigative label without much discrimination—it has a modish ring and makes a news show sound aggressive—but that shouldn't frighten anyone off. It is also the style of the moment to ask questions in a tough, belligerent manner to convey the impression that the newsman isn't letting the subject get away with anything. That fashion of interviewing was made irresistibly popular by *60 Minutes,* and its imitators will probably be with us for some years. But that is a matter of style, not substance.

While there are exceptions, I find the news media in this country rather deferential to business. That is probably a reflection of the fact that the American psyche is rather hospitable to business. Nowhere is the making of things and their buying and selling considered a more worthy and respectable occupation of man's energies than in the United States. And the media reflect that underlying belief, even if they seem to growl at every businessman they see.

I was impressed several years ago by this observation from Daniel Patrick Moynihan, scholar, presidential adviser, U.N. Ambassador, now U.S. Senator from New York:

ON TELEVISION!

The American business system went on doing tolerably well, or better than that, but proved wholly incapable of making a case for itself. It did justifiable things. It could not justify them. It did admirable things. It could not make them seem admirable.

To remedy that, American business clearly needs greater sophistication in handling the media, which will deliver its message and convey its image. The medium that will reach the greatest number of people is television, and this book will certainly help make its readers more sophisticated in using television and understanding it.

PREFACE

This book grew out of several experiences by the authors—as coach, player, and spectator. In 1971 Jack Hilton began a TV course for an advertising agency. In 1976 he went on his own as a television consultant, and by 1980 he had trained some 15,000 corporate executives in the sport of the broadcast interview through intensive one- and two-day sessions in videotape studios where students learned how to fend off leading questions, handle difficult situations, and win by getting their points across no matter what obstacles a show or host raised. What they learned will help them and their companies present an accurate or a better television face. On the side it taught those executives how to apply what they learned to the community projects they volunteered for after hours.

That's how this book came about. Do you want to tell your story on television or radio? Do you want to know when and what to believe when you watch or listen to a talk show? Maybe you're just interested in how it all works. That's what this book intends to explain, and if at some time you should need to put this information to use, it's all laid out.

Why should people, in business particularly, know anything about television and how it works? Because sooner or later they will have to make use of it.

Public access to the broadcast media is a growing issue. In some areas where cable television is a reality, public access is a reality. More and more Americans are going to find themselves in the position of spokesman or spokeswoman as this trend continues. Now, at least, they don't have to learn by doing. Learning by doing on television is disaster for most people anyhow. The technological revolution that has made business as dependent on computers as it once was on typewriters continues to change the way businesses are conducted. And television, both in its form as an information-disseminating medium and as a tool for business communication, is in the forefront of the technologies that change the way American business goes about its job.

It began with the necessity for business to explain itself to the public, and it will continue to insert itself into the inner workings of business as the 1980s increase the need for speedy communication and decision making. Closed circuit television systems will replace face-to-face meetings, just as videotape technology has revolutionized employee training and education. Even before that turn of events, however, business people, particularly those high in the corporate ranks, will find themselves more and more in demand as news interview subjects and television show participants. To wait until a company or organization makes news is dangerous, just as it was dangerous for blacksmiths to pooh-pooh the infernal automobile. Television exposure has great power to enhance or damage a company's reputation, and the executive who fails to prepare for his turn in the camera's eye is courting disaster.

This book will look at the enormous impact television has on the public's perception of business and other American institutions, how reputations can be made or muddied through the eye of a television camera. If a businessman or woman is still skeptical after reading it, let him or her consider the object lessons provided by those who let television come to them without preparation. Like the computer revolution, the television revolution will have its share of victims long before it will have its converts.

Television has long had its place as a tool for selling products, but too few people have considered its power to sell personalities and ideas, to shape public opinion favorably or unfavorably toward institutions and individuals. By dissecting the television information process, we like to think that more people will become sophisticated users and viewers of the images transmitted daily to millions of American homes.

Jack Hilton
Mary Knoblauch

ACKNOWLEDGMENTS

Like all books this one is the work of many people. The authors worked on it for a couple of years, but it probably wouldn't have been completed without the help of confidants and friends from the outside worlds of television, the press, and professional communications. Among the most helpful were John Boomer, Susan Chamberlain, Ray D'Argenio, Bob Elliott, Ramon Greenwood, Dennis Israel, Peter Jacobi, Dallas Kersey, Harry Levine, Jim Morakis, Edwin Newman, John Penicnak, and George Reedy.

No book is likely to be successful unless its editor has worked as hard as its authors did, if not as long. Natalie Meadow was our editor, and did she ever!

The final truth is that few books even get to an editor without the help of first-class secretaries like Barbara Zielinski and Hilary Marcus, neither of whom is available for hire (except by us).

To all of the above—many thanks!

CONTENTS

CONTENTS

EPIGRAPH

Guests on discussion/interview programs and members of the public who participate in phone-in programs shall be treated with due respect by the program host/hostess.

Interview/discussion programs, including telephone participation programs, should be governed by accepted standards of ethical journalism.

Any agreement substantively limiting areas of discussion/questions should be announced at the outset of the program.

From the Radio Code
of the National Association
of Broadcasters

CHAPTER 1

THE RISE
OF GUERRILLAS

In the beginning, when people first learned to talk, spreading the news was a simple matter of passing on the day's events in front of a communal campfire. When Og played up his role in the hunt a bit beyond tolerance, Uk had his say at the evening fire, and if it took a bump on the head for Og to admit his mistake, well, the fairness doctrine had its way of setting the record straight even then.

Tens of thousands of years later, the situation is much the same, except that the newsmakers talk from a box in the living room and the fire stays in the furnace where it belongs, or acts as decoration in a fireplace. Between the beginning and now, keeping

1

an eye on important events became more difficult. The printing press eased matters, but the growth of civilization around the world revised the "need to know" concept. For a while, if a person knew what was going on in his village, it was enough. Then if he knew what was going on in his region, his kingdom, or even his part of the continent, that was enough.

And now—well, even the village is a pretty big place to keep track of. And it's not just a matter of government in Washington affecting gas pumps in Seattle—it's civil wars in remote countries that can have a serious impact on people halfway around the world. It's scientific research in Boston that could wipe out a city—or prolong the average lifespan by 20 years if enough money could become available to finish the project.

No one person can keep up with the news without help. It's a function that has to be delegated to someone else, to someone we can trust to sift through the tens of thousands of books, thousands of magazines, the miles of reports and wire service stories, the endless hours of conversations with powerful and wise and idiotic news shapers to get at the absolutely important facts and trends we need to know to make it through another day.

The "someone" we trust is a mysterious entity called "the media," frequently used in a singular sense, as if it really "is" a person. But it takes at least two mediums to make the media. Within the medium of television, there are three networks, and within each network there are a couple of hundred affiliates, and within each affiliate, which is a station to most people, there are individual news and information shows, run by people of varying talents who must decide every day what goes on the schedule. In the end, although this is not a comfortable thing for any of these people to acknowledge, they often don't know a hell of a lot more about what the audience wants or needs than the audience, sitting in front of its living-room box, does.

Like the audience at home, they are dependent on *their* media—the network news structure, the wire services, government and corporation spokesmen—all of them populated with individuals who have different ideas about what the client at home needs to know.

What the media people *do* know, however, is what to do with the tools of their trade, and just in case the medium they work for is lacking, they invite the audience to venture into other media for balance. Television people, who right now work for the number one medium in the country, often advise the audience to read newspapers for the "complete story." Newspapers and magazines operate on the assumption that they are bringing the second word on a subject—after television. And radio assumes its audience is fickle, turning elsewhere after a half hour or so, so they repeat everything at regular intervals. Knowing the tools of the trade, media people also know their limitations.

And very humanly, they work from strength. Over the past fifteen years, the sophistication of the tools has increased so much that the flashy effects they can achieve outweigh the content they deliver. An untrained person venturing before the camera to tell his or her story can easily fall victim to the medium. And without telling the story on television, the person may never get that story across to the audience. This dilemma brought the rise of the television guerrilla, who learned enough about the medium to use it for

3

his own purposes. That is not as diabolical as it may seem. We send our children to school to learn to read and write so they can be informed and can communicate with others. But in an age of electronic communication, reading and writing isn't enough. You have to know how to see, and perhaps be seen; how to listen, and perhaps how to talk into a microphone.

These days, a guerrilla guide to television may be as important as learning to read, because Americans get more information from the living-room box than anywhere else. Television isn't always fair or truthful. It doesn't always tell you what you need to know, and despite all the editorial replies and fairness provisions, mistakes are still made, either because people don't know how to correct them or because they don't know how to fight back.

Now they can learn.

CHAPTER 2

ELECTRONIC LITERACY

At various times in human history, whole classes, whole sexes, and whole peoples have been denied access to the tools of communication. In many civilizations, the skill of reading has been confined to a few, whose special knowledge allowed them to rule without interference.

Literacy and access to knowledge available through print and books have caused more than one revolution. Print literacy for centuries has been a means for the powerless or poor to gain power and wealth by educating themselves in new skills or by acquiring basic knowledge. Within the memory of many Americans are the infamous literacy tests of the

5

South, which effectively blocked black voters from the polls for many years.

But the electronic media have replaced print as the basic source of information in this country, and the ordinary person is severely limited in the ability to get before a microphone and camera. In fact, even the extraordinary person has found it difficult to reach an electronic forum with regularity. The President of the United States is the only significant exception.

Sometime in the next decade all that will begin to change, as television in new forms becomes accessible to vast numbers of Americans for purposes quite different from the news and entertainment mix we now consume on the major networks. In many areas of the country, cable television has already opened new outlets for broadcasters and viewers, and pay cable programming has widened the entertainment choices for those to whom it is available. Pay cable, such as Home Box Office, offers original concerts recorded solely for cable customers, and the full capacity of cable television, where it exists, has opened the door to nearly anyone who can find his or her way to the studio where community-access programs are produced.

Videotape recorders, still in their infancy, are opening a market for prerecorded videotaped programs whose potential would seem to be endless, even if the programs so far are nothing more than a merchandising gimmick to attract buyers of blank tape. The day is not far off when a company will produce a videotape program for the home recorder, sold to home users at a slight discount for one viewing and erasure. Even more economical in the future is the infant videodisc industry. Videodisc players, like record players, can play back inexpensive videorecordings on vinyl discs, although they cannot record programs. The discs are so inexpensive to manufacture—the cost is measured in cents rather than the dollars of videotape—that once established, it is possible that disc systems will outpace tape systems in the long run.

And there are the communication satellites. Barely into puberty as a technology, the satellites orbiting the earth are used to process long-distance telephone calls and to extend television signals to remote areas of the world. Countries can contract with Comsat and the National Aeronautics and Space Administration to put a satellite into a precise orbit over a country, giving instant multichannel access to television in the middle of the Sahara Desert.

A television set in a home in an ordinary market uses a mere fraction of the available channels. As the satellite systems proliferate, more and more of these channels will become available to a single set, multiplying the choice of programming and adding new voices to the electronic spectrum. One of the most interesting satellite experiments is run by Ted Turner, who has set up an operation that transmits certain local independent television stations' programming and a 24-hour news service to cable television subscribers around the country. Religious television networks operate the same way. Ohters are following almost weekly.

Satellites are on the verge of making the ordinary business meeting an anachronism. It is now possible in selected cities to go to a telephone company meeting room and be hooked up visually and audibly with a meeting room in another city. The efficiency of this system is irresistible, even if you consider only the hours saved in travel and the general wear and tear on participants. And disregard the advantage of speeding decision making. Combining such a system with existing telecopying systems even allows documents to change hands during the course of such an electronic meeting. Eventually all companies and organizations of any size will have their own satellite channel or channels, their own transponders for direct communication through the satellite, and the peripheral cameras and telecopiers. The space shuttle will make new satellite placement routine; the increased cost and scarcity of automobile and airplane fuel will make such systems cost-efficient in short time.

If you are thirty years old, in business or the professions, the chances of your avoiding an appearance on television in the next twenty years are nearly zero. The audience for your television show may be small—six colleagues in another city, twenty-five salesmen in the Atlanta office, one director in each of six cities. But you will be on television.

For many people such appearances will become as routine as a face-to-face meeting. Some people will take advantage of the medium instinctively, but unfortunately many will not realize the subtle and dangerous differences between talking to a camera and talking face to face until it is too late.

When you are in a face-to-face meeting with a group of people around a conference table, you do not look at all of them at the same time. Your eyes are like a camera tracking from one to the other, or focused on a single speaker or a single participant. Your companions are doing the same; some may not be looking at anyone at all. But when you are in an electronic meeting with your participants lined up with equal prominence on a projection television screen in front of you, you will look at the scene differently. While you are watching the president make a key point you will also see that Joe over there looks bored. Your eyes are focused on the entire image, not on a single object. You are seeing more than you would ordinarily.

A camera—especially one that has closeup powers—changes the viewer's perception. If you were sitting in an ordinary room attentively watching a speaker, he or she would be at some physical distance from you, anywhere from four feet away across a desk to twenty feet away at the other end of the conference room. But a television camera in closeup can move that person's face to an electronic distance physically equivalent to a nose-to-nose confrontation. If you were to speak to a person with your noses touching in a face-to-face meeting, you wouldn't see any more than you see when you kiss someone with your eyes wide open. When a television camera does the equivalent of that closeup, you get a perspective you can never have in real life. *It changes reality.* You see things in a person's face you never saw before. You get clues to the person's state of mind that would be hidden at ordinary physical distances. And because of this artificial perspective, participants in an electronic meeting can inadvertently send and receive signals that were never intended.

The importance of this distinction is magnified by yet another experimental television system. Qube, a two-way television communication system, is expanding slowly from its first test market in Columbus, Ohio. The system, operated by Warner Communications, allows viewers to respond to what they see on television. They can order items they see in commercials, they can vote on issues raised in discussion and news shows, and they can even influence programming by expressing approval or disapproval of a show on request.

With television a familiar presence in 97 percent of American households, how farfetched is a presidential election within the next two decades where the voters never leave their homes? Or a local election. Or a referendum.

In recent years executives and aspirants to high political office have become aware of the need to have a good television presence. They have learned that if they don't use the medium, it will use them. President Carter has a media adviser ensconced in the White House, as all presidents since Dwight Eisenhower have had. Certainly no future president would be without a staff adviser for television.

The need to understand television's quirks, the tricks it plays, and the changes in emphasis it makes is not exactly a national obsession. People are not clamoring for lessons in electronic literacy as their forebears clamored for the right to read. Not yet, anyhow. So far, only those who have suffered the damage television can wreak on an amateur understand the need for electronic literacy. And it may be that open access to electronic literacy may not come until ignorance has created a national disaster. Even now the ability of a trained television communicator to sway an audience to his opinion is a real danger. As politicians fight more and more of their campaign battles on the airwaves, it becomes important for the audience to be able to separate style from substance, to see the tricks of the trade for what they are.

Early in our reading years, we run across our first instance of a lie committed in print. It can be devastating to learn that these magic things called words can be used to deceive as well as to reveal, yet somehow we have become inured to the risks, because day after day we electronic illiterates allow a minority of literate electronic professionals to bend our opinions and shape our thoughts. The reins of the Federal Communications Commission are loose at best, and organized citizen protests are pretty much limited to sex and violence and the advertising aimed at children.

Perhaps we need to teach people how to watch. It is just as important for the audience to know the ins and outs of the medium as it is for a person appearing on television. If the public remains passive, we may recreate in modern-day terms the situation of the Middle Ages, when the monks kept their knowledge locked in the exclusive club of those who read Latin while the populace knew only what the keepers of knowledge wanted them to know.

Today we insist that our educated citizenry have a working knowledge of our language and its powers. When students show a decline in language skills, it is cause for national alarm. Yet not once in an ordinary person's education (except for those bound for the priesthood of employment in the electronic media) is there a course on how to appear on or react to television. At best, students get a course in public speaking, modestly evolved from the days when people orated without benefit of microphone—a far cry from what is needed. How does that equip them to deal intelligently with a presidential campaign debate on television? How will they decide which button to push on the Qube control box when it comes to their living rooms?

Today's students, pouring out of high schools and

colleges, have far more chance of conducting at least a portion of their important business in front of a camera than they do of publishing words or orating before a large live audience. And for sure, they will spend as many hours devouring the product of television as they do at anything else, with the possible exception of sleeping.

Television as we know it has evolved from the theater and the movies, and therefore its show business quotient is high. But there are certain elements that make television work differently from its forebears, too. If enough people understood its nature and limitations, it would be possible to set down some true guidelines on how television should operate to help its audience learn and its practition-ers communicate. Without that knowledgeable audi-ence, however, television will continue to muddle along as a tool of the initiates.

Ideally this book, which is designed to teach people how to use television, will also raise some debate on how the medium can and should serve people.

CHAPTER 3

WHO DO YOU TRUST?

That marvelously ungrammatical title launched
Johnny Carson on television as a quiz show host.
A comedian with a gift for ad libs, Carson has spent
nearly two decades as the foremost talk-show host on
television. Night after night he gives millions of
Americans a look at the people behind show
business names. Sprinkled among them are occasional authors, scientists, politicians, and crusaders
whom Carson interviews. Many of them make news
and are interviewed elsewhere by "real" newsmen
and women as subjects of newspaper profiles and
magazine covers. Despite an apparent erosion in the
Tonight Show's ratings, a smart newsmaker would

give up three magazines and four *Issues and Answers* for 15 minutes on the Carson show.

Carson's show and its audience are unique. Coming at the end of the broadcast day, just before bedtime, it reaches Americans at their most receptive. If Johnny finds a subject interesting, very likely they will too. They know Carson from hundreds of hours he has visited with them in their living rooms or bedrooms. They *trust* him, and by inference they trust his guests.

In many ways Johnny Carson's *Tonight Show* is the essence of television. It has a comfortable familiarity—the opening monolog, the banter with Ed McMahon, the steady progression of guests in 10- to 15-minute segments. Predictable, but seldom dull. Interesting, but not taxing. Voluble, but not controversial. If you can't trust Carson, who can you trust?

So people trust him, as they trust television. In 1959, The Roper Organization completed the first research report measuring "Trends in Public Attitudes Toward Television and Other Mass Media." It asked people: "Where do you usually get most of your news about what's going on in the world today?" The basic choices were newspapers, radio, television, magazines, and talking to other people. Newspapers won with 57 percent. Television was second with 51 percent. (Some people gave more than one answer.) Radio was third with 34 percent, and magazines scored only 8 percent.

Four years later, television took the lead and has held it throughout the eleven surveys Roper has conducted. The most recent, in late 1978, gave television 67 percent of the vote. Only 49 percent voted for newspapers as a basic news source.

The Roper Organization survey asked another

illuminating question: "If you get conflicting or different reports of the same news story from radio, television, the magazines, and the newspapers, which of the four versions would you be most inclined to believe?" In 1978, 47 percent voted for television, and only 23 percent said newspapers—a two-to-one advantage.

It has become fashionable for print people, even beyond newspaper and magazine writers, to denigrate the enemy by denigrating its audience. Advertising man Jerry Della Femina, who wrote a popular book about advertising, characterized viewers this way: "Your real beer drinker can sit home watching television and polish off two six-packs a night," he wrote in *From Those Wonderful Folks Who Gave You Pearl Harbor.** "If he's thirsty, or it's hot out, make that even more. His wife will drink only four or five cans because she's suddenly decided that she really shouldn't drink more than a six-pack a night—it won't look good. So you've got like three six-packs a family a night. And you can count their kid in if he's over ten years old."

There's your audience for television, right? A fantastic unwashed multitude ripe for a new detergent or pantyhose that won't sag, but certainly not an audience for people whose product is ideas or whose mission is changing opinions. Maybe such stereotypes make print people feel better, but they are hardly accurate. Almost everyone in the United States watches television, except for those few souls who live in tiny towns ringed with mountains that cut off TV reception. (They are such an oddity that they make good features on network TV news shows.) The

*New York: Simon & Schuster, 1970.

curmudgeons who ritualistically throw out their sets are an equally small minority.

The rest of America, whether educated at Harvard and postgraduated at Yale or functionally illiterate and unemployed, watches the tube. "Suppose that you could continue to have only *one* of the following," Roper's poll asked. "Radio, television, newspapers, or magazines; which one would you *most* want to *keep*?" Television, said 45 percent of the college-educated in 1974. Only 26 percent of the college graduates voted for newspapers.

Ah, but *rich* people don't watch television, the snipers will argue. Roper sampled "upper economic levels" in 1974, too, defined as "the top 25 percent of the sample in income." Among those, 54 percent wouldn't hear of parting with TV. Only 25 percent preferred a newspaper. The rich watch TV as well as the poor, the educated as well as the unschooled. In 1978, the college crowd had a median daily viewing time of 2 hours, 31 minutes. The rich had a median of 2 hours, 52 minutes. The national median then was 3 hours, 8 minutes. Every day.

Who do they all trust? Television, particularly its news and information shows. The commercials and prime-time entertainment programming are another matter, but because there is a differentiation between them and news shows ("This program was produced by NBC News, which is solely responsible for its content"), viewers have come to the conclusion that what they see on the news and public affairs shows can *really* be trusted. You can *see* the spokesman talking. You can *hear* the company president explain his position. In a newspaper, the reader has to rely on the writer to interpret an interview for him. But on television, the viewer can watch the person's face. He observes telltale signs of uncertainty, picks up word inflections (something that made the Watergate tapes so difficult for the average newspaper reader to decipher), and he forms impressions about the personalities he has watched.

The truth is that the camera and the microphone are not always accurate. That sweaty, shifty-eyed person being interviewed may not be a lying scoundrel, only a poor soul unschooled in television and in such an agony of stagefright that his mind is in danger of going as blank as a new videotape. As a result, a viewer may reach totally erroneous and unjustified conclusions. On the other side of the coin are those who *do* know all the tricks and can occasionally make the most outrageous untruths sound like direct communications from the deity. Those are extreme cases, but viewers' conclusions about them are just as erroneous.

In the vast majority of talk shows, of news interviews, of panel discussions, those who know how to use the medium come out looking better and more convincing than those who don't know how to use it. In this world of ours, style can mean as much as an opinion itself. The news and discussion programs on television have a show business aspect, too. The director chooses the camera angles, the interviewer asks the questions he wants to ask, and the editor on a filmed or taped show can restructure everything to produce a result none of the participants ever intended. To be in control of the situation is the ideal, and few Americans get a chance to do that.

In *Conversations with Kennedy*,* Benjamin Brad-lee of the Washington Post recalls his friendship with

*New York: W. W. Norton & Co., 1975.

the late President. One entry from his diary, dated December 17, 1962, is illuminating:

The President went on television *live* tonight, answering questions from each network's White House correspondent—Sander Vanocur of NBC, Bill Lawrence of ABC (both friends of Kennedy), and George Herman of CBS.

I watched it at home, and felt professionally threatened as a man who was trying to make a living by the written word. The program was exceptionally good, well-paced, colorful, humorous, serious, and I felt that a written account would have paled by comparison. After it was over I called Kennedy to tell him all this.

"Well," he told me, "I always said that *when we don't have to go through you bastards, we can really get our story over to the American people.*" (Italics ours.)

In somewhat saltier language, President Kennedy was saying the same thing anybody with an opinion to air or an idea to circulate has concluded: When you want a mass audience, and you want it to believe what you say, no vehicle is as good as television.

Provided you are in control. At least some of the time.

That brings us back to the *Tonight Show.* One of the things that makes it an ideal vehicle for a nonperforming guest is that Carson is invariably gracious to his "serious guests." By and large they come on last, and with only 12 minutes or so to go, Carson dispenses with the bantering and lets the guest say his or her piece. His questions elicit information—for the most part, the exact information the guest wants to give out. And if the guest isn't a total nervous wreck, his message is conveyed to

18

millions. He couldn't hope to accomplish that by any other method.

The *Tonight Show* is not a news program. It comes under the entertainment arm of NBC, where the guest concept is taken somewhat more literally than it is on good news and interview shows on and off the networks. There the rules of the ring apply. And sometimes fair play is suspended. If you know the rules and the ways to break them, you can defend yourself against an unfair opponent. If you're a spectator at the sport, knowing the rules makes it all that much more fun to watch. And if you'd like to play the game, it helps to take lessons.

CHAPTER 4

WHO ARE THESE GUYS, ANYHOW?

Although it is beginning to change, many of the men and women who host the nation's islands of television talk have no special training for their jobs. Much of what they do day in and day out or week in and week out they have learned through trial and error, or by watching and listening to those who originally shaped the form of television and radio news and talk formats for the networks. Some of them learned well, some heard only the cadences or saw only the surface poise of their role models, but most, especially in the smaller markets, learned one or two very basic formats into which every interview must fit.

"Ladies and gentlemen, our guest this afternoon

is Mr. Adams, who is here to tell us about his new book, *How to Make Your Life Work for You from the Birth Canal On.* That's a very unusual title, Mr. Adams. Could you tell us how you settled on the birth canal as a beginning?" It is unlikely that the interviewer has read the book; if he had, his introduction would set up the thesis of the book for the audience. It is, however, very nice for Mr. Adams, who will communicate exactly what he wishes the audience to think about his book without fear of interruption. The approach is kindly, almost deferential, hardly designed to terrify the subject.

Even in a news interview, a reporter will usually settle on the basic informational questions he or she learned in an elementary reporting course. "Tell us, Mrs. Stanley, *who* was the victim? *What* was he doing in the massage parlor when the fire broke out? *Where* were you when the fire started? *When* did you begin working for Friendly Fingers? *Why* do you think the victim ran back into the burning building when the police and fire trucks arrived? *How* did the fire start, do you think?" It's not fancy, it's not inventive, but it works.

Compared with a network correspondent or a network talk-show host, these people are the galley slaves of the broadcast business. In addition to the interview with Mr. Adams, that noon talk-show host may have production duties and other chores around the station that are his or her real job. The talk show is an added duty thrown to an ambitious person whose real desire is to be an on-air personality. There simply isn't time to prepare. Or that person may be a broadcast amateur who made his or her reputation years ago in community theater, whence he or she was plucked to do the noon show.

That reporter may have four other stories to cover before rushing back to the studio to edit the film and tape in time for the evening newscast. Any thinking the reporter does is going on during the interview itself. He has arrived perhaps 10 minutes before, with just enough time to sketch in the broadest details of the fire before he had to start asking questions for the camera. Although these people may sound more relaxed than their subjects, the demands of their job provide for little more than a surface once-over of the physical facts of the story.

Faced with a knowledgeable interviewee, such a reporter can only defer to the person with greater knowledge of the subject at hand. And unless you happen to be talking about a subject that was his or her minor in college or is by chance an avocation pursued on the run by an overworked host or reporter, the chances of your being embarrassed by the fine points of the interviewer's knowledgeable questions are slim indeed.

Charles Kuralt, who has spent a decade doing *On The Road* for CBS News, has probably seen more boondock television than anybody else, one motel at a time. "My overwhelming impression of all those hours in all those years is of hair," he reports. "Anchormen's hair. Hair carefully styled and sprayed, hair neatly parted, hair abundant, and every hair in place. There's a big improvement in hair styles, but I can't remember much that came out from beneath all that hair. And I fear that the reason may be there wasn't much substance there. I am ashamed, I think we all ought be ashamed, that twenty-five years into the television age, so many of our anchormen haven't any basis on which to make a news judgment, can't edit, can't write, and can't cover a story."

Ted Baxter, the dippy anchorman on the *Mary Tyler Moore Show,* has counterparts across the country. The news at 6 P.M. on one big city TV station had been done every night for several years by a newscaster we'll call Tom Swift. It was sponsored by Shell. Each night Swift would stare into the camera at the appointed hour and say: "Good evening. The six o'clock news is brought to you by Shell. I'm Tom Swift."

To jog his memory, those simple sentences were lettered on an "idiot card," which the floor director would hold up next to the camera *to be read verbatim* night after night, on instructions from Shell's advertising agency. (Idiot cards are aptly named.)

One night Tom Swift was sick and didn't show up for work. Designated to replace him at 6 P.M. was a newscaster we'll call Ted Baxter, who happened to be loitering in the announcers' lounge, impeccably groomed, magnificently tailored, and marvelously powdered. Ted always *smelled* so good, the importance of which is difficult to measure over television and radio.

Replacing Tom was no problem for Ted, since his own show, the 6:30 news on the radio side, never required his attention until 15 seconds beforehand. At 30 seconds before 6 P.M., Ted Baxter stormed through the corridor toward the studio, still shuffling his copy, handed to him moments before by a harried, harassed news writer. Ten seconds before six, he bolted into the studio, took his position behind Tom's lectern, and clipped a microphone to his tie just in time to see the tally light blaze on the camera in front of him. The floor director, idiot cards in position, threw the cue.

"Good evening," said Ted Baxter, looking straight

23

'You have a smudge on your nose.'

into the camera. "The six o'clock news is brought to you by Shell. I'm Tom Swift."

Just like his namesake, Ted looked disconcerted, but only for an instant. Composure restored, he made his best attempt to save the day.

"Oh, swell," he said.

Then he read the news.

It may be hard to understand why the journalism schools, which teach broadcast journalism, and the radio and television stations, which use the talents of their students, have not found a solution to the Ted Baxter problem, particularly in an era when television is not only influential but wealthy.

Many of the schools are hampered by out-of-date equipment to such a degree that no matter how well their students are trained as journalists, they frequently have little opportunity to experiment in front of the camera and even less idea how the modern news-gathering technology operates until they land their first job. And that entry-level job requires them to follow the direction of people who themselves have had little or no time to ponder a better way to use the Minicam and other tools of the medium. By default, too often, the old, safe ways of handling information prevail, and the Ted Baxters remain the role models for new staffers.

It may be hard to understand why some stations are so concerned with appearance at the expense of good communication. Perhaps it helps to remember that radio and television stations are not run by people whose primary objective is improving the flow of information. The stations are businesses, and highly profitable ones at that, headed most often by someone who rose through the money ranks and not the news and information ranks. Operating profits border on the unconscionable or the euphoric, depending on your point of view. There is no reason to change the status quo so long as the money is rolling in, a fact the occasional crusader for better TV news learns the hard way.

It's important to keep this profile of the local station in mind, because, to begin with, at least, most television guerrillas are going to be fighting in those small jungles, not in the network big time. Obviously more people can take a hand in local or regional issues than in national causes. And even if the cause is national, you're going to spend much more time on the air if you stick with the smaller places than if you go for the *Today* show and the Big Apple.

There may seem to be a certain "gong show" mentality in broadcasting, a tendency to give precedence to the flamboyant personality or the oddball idea, rather than to the mainstream opinion. That's true. What's the point of having someone on to defend the state of good health? If everyone agrees that red lights mean stop, there is no point in inviting an advocate of red lights to appear on a talk show. Now if you can find an advocate of fuchsia lights—assuming there is some reasonable explanation for this passion—that's news. News talks about change; it upsets the status quo. The more people you want to rattle by your proposal, the more likely it is that you will get a microphone to say your piece. And if your idea won't upset a lot of people but is quirky (like the tongue-in-cheek campaign to put diapers on animals), you'll get on. Broadcasters and other journalists look for the news in a situation. It's not enough to say you want to get on a show to talk about the state of street paving. Tell them what you think should be done, and if your ideas are news, you'll make it.

Remember, the men who drafted the Constitution considered the press an institution that would challenge authority, be undisciplined, even somewhat irresponsible. And now it has its own set of checks and balances in the broadcast version. All those wild-eyed hosts and writers and seekers-of-change work for bosses who are determined not to rock the profit boat.

CHAPTER 5

WHEN IS TELEVISION NECESSARY?

Sometimes you don't have any choice in the matter. If you are the victim of a spectacular crime or disaster, television will make that decision for you. If you are a banker, and an employee embezzles a six-figure sum, television will make room for your face and voice. But when you are trying to *make* news, it's you who decides when television is necessary.

Some things are easier to sell than others. If you are promoting some local good cause with a hot-air-balloon race, all you have to do is let the assignment desks at the various television stations near you know the time and place, and they'll fall all over themselves trying to get there early. The same is true of a kite fly, a massive egg roll, a sailboat race, or a skate-in for charity. Each of those events has a high visual factor, and television news programs rely on visual stories to keep their news shows going between the nuts and bolts of talking heads. That's why fires get such extraordinary play on television, even when the building in question is a deserted, collapsing warehouse in some nook of the city no one ever heard of. If a crew can get there while the flames are still shooting skyward, it is a shoo-in on the news.

So if the story you are trying to tell has a visual content, start with the news department of a television station. It doesn't have to be something as spectacular as a balloon race. Let's say your local school is in desperate need of tuck-pointing—so desperate that a child can pull a piece of brick out by hand. You are on a committee trying to get a badly needed school bond issue passed in the face of a tax rebellion by the electorate. School bonds and rebellious taxpayers are not very sexy, but the sight of an eight-year-old prying a brick from a structurally unsafe building makes a dramatic point, and in exchange, the news crew will allow you a few words on camera to explain how the bond issue will make this building safe for the children. You get what you want; they get what they want.

Armed with that experience, you can call the producer of a local talk show and probably sell him or her on a slot to talk about how unsafe the buildings are. Once there, you can pitch your bond issue.

Sometimes the cause you are peddling is merely a smokescreen for something else. Let's say you are a lawyer with political ambitions in your local mayoralty race two years from now. Your name is not exactly a household word yet, and attempting to get air time under your true colors is fruitless. But there is nothing to stop you from taking up the cudgel for some issue around which you intend to base your forthcoming campaign. You form a citizens committee for honesty in government, or a citizens committee to build a new stadium, or a citizens committee to improve the parks and playgrounds. Find a dramatic way to demonstrate the problem and you're flying.

This is not to suggest that everyone who forms a citizens committee has ulterior motives, but it does illustrate how a very personal goal (being mayor) can be transformed into an issue that affects a great many people.

By and large when you want to use the power of television to communicate, you must demonstrate that your cause is of interest or benefit to a great many people. But a worthy cause is not enough in itself. You must have something new to say about the subject, something you have discovered yourself, engineered yourself, or dramatized in a newsworthy fashion. Tradition may get you a berth on a talk show without that piece of news, but it won't get or keep the audience's attention at home, and that's what you're really after.

This becomes particularly hard when your cause is some annual event. One woman, faced with promoting an auction to benefit the orchestra in a small city, found herself with none of the auction items at hand as she pitched herself to a television talk show. Instead, she did her homework on the diminishing funding available to arts organizations across the country and was able to plead the cause of the annual auction with eloquence.

Ultimately, the importance of your cause is less important than the style in which you sell it. If you are an original personality, you may not need much of a cause to get a talk-show berth. But if you aren't, there are ways to sell your cause anyhow, sometimes even when there is no news.

1. Is there a way to demonstrate a perceived benefit to many people from your cause? (The benefit need only be perceived, not real.)

2. Is there a way to package your cause that makes it *seem* new, even if it's old? (A more recent set of statistics can do the job.)

3. Is there a dramatic way to illustrate your cause, even if your message is decades old? (Charts, films, slides, testimonials.)

4. Can you demonstrate a particular expertise in talking about a subject of continuing public interest? (A favorite ploy of physicians, lawyers, and other professionals who are not permitted to advertise widely, but who like broadcast exposure as a way to build a practice.)

Why go to all that trouble? Because you want to communicate with a great many people. It doesn't matter if your motive is selfish; what matters is that you want to reach as large an audience as possible. If that is your goal, television is your medium, and you'll figure out a way to sell yourself.

CHAPTER 6

HOW TO GET ON THE AIR

There's always the simplest procedure: you call up the host and ask if you can be on the show. If the host won't talk to you, speak to the producer. If the show prefers its requests from guests in writing, keep it to one page of typing, with just a few clippings attached to help support your point or your credibility. Follow that up with a phone call. Don't call later than an hour before the show goes on the air. After that point, the host and staff will be too busy to talk. And after the show the host is as wrung out as you will be after your performance, definitely not in the mood to hear about the school bond issue.

Simple as this procedure is, it has its pitfalls, so

do your homework first. In any given market there may be two to twenty alternatives to choose from, some of them shows with definite subject limitations. For example, it would not be smart to argue the cause of a community theater on the 5 A.M. outdoor and fishing talk show. But it might work very nicely on a local issues talk show on your educational television station. Sell yourself to the slot that looks most logical. That may mean combing your local TV magazine to cull all the talk shows in the schedule. Don't let 2 A.M. time slots bother you—those shows are usually pretaped at a civilized hour. Do the same with the radio stations. If your local newspaper doesn't print full radio schedules, you may have to do some listening around the dial to find your target. It's worth the effort.

In your peregrinations around the channel selector and across the AM and FM dials, try not to let the commercials be your guide. The host can't help what the sales department sells, and most stations these days require advertisers to buy their ads "run-of-station," particularly on radio. This means that the advertiser's four commercials per day will run sometime in that twenty-four-hour period, but not always in the time slots of the advertiser's or host's choosing.

If you are going to do one of those 2 A.M. talk shows on television, and the ads are all for TV offerings of somebody's greatest hits or kitchen gadget marvels, you can assume that the rates at this hour are somewhat lower than usual, and that the audience at home is equivalently smaller. This should not sway you in a choice of debut, but you should be aware that a berth on such a show will not get your message across to the multitudes. It is, however, a good place to practice before you take your act on the road to the higher rated shows in better time slots.

When you've found a likely show, listen to it a few times before you call. Familiarity can breed respect from the host.

If you have your own PR rep, it's easier, so long as the rep approaches the project in the same spirit. Barry Farber, a talk-show host on WMCA radio in New York City, wrote his guide, "How *Not* to Get on the Barry Farber Show," in the hope of educating the public relations fraternity:

When calling to pitch one of your clients for an interview, do not begin by asking, "Are you still on the air?"

If for some reason you insist on that opening above all others, at least don't sound so incredulous when we reply in the affirmative.

I will (according to which is most appropriate) congratulate, kiss, or marry the first PR person who says, "Look, a great talker he's not, but he's got a lot of important information a lesser interviewer than you couldn't possibly elicit."

Don't ask, "How long is he going to be on?" It's like lovemaking. We'll both know 10 seconds before it's over.

Having promised me a guest who will strike down my competitors with terminal envy, and who thereupon starts out weak and gradually tapers off, do not (while I am applying mouth-to-mouth resuscitation, feeling for his pulse, and signaling the engineer to hurry in with his harmonica) tell me about *another* one of your clients who's even better!

I *know* how clients are. I *know* you're in a "You-furnish-the-fleet, we'll-furnish-the-ocean" business. Nevertheless, in dealing with us, bear in mind: honesty is always one of the alternatives.

Farber speaks for more than himself. Be honest about why you want to be on the show, what you have to offer, and what you cannot supply. If none of this strikes the host's fancy, ask why. There may be a good reason, or you may just have struck out. If the host has a reason, listen to it carefully. If he or she has no reason, ask if you can rethink it and call or write again. Do not, however, ask the host to recommend another show or approach for you. It's not their business to act as your public relations counsel, and making the request is a professional insult, implying you weren't really after the host's show after all.

The exceptionally confident guerrilla may have a friend or connection at the station in question, a big advertiser. If getting on the show means more to you than anything else, ask the advertiser to put pressure on the host through the sales department. You are guaranteed a hostile host, but if you are positive you can handle the situation, go ahead and pull your strings.

CHAPTER 7

I'LL BE
CHEWED UP

Possible, but not likely, unless your cause is putting pornography into the elementary school curriculum. People who get chewed up in an interview can't blame their inexperience. They have broken the rules, aggravated the host past tolerance, or have simply been scared to death. Just because you've never done an interview show, in fact, the host is likely to give you at least initial aid and comfort, provided you are a responsible human being talking knowledgeably about a subject of interest.

Even Mike Wallace, the acknowledged master of intimidation, generally saves his big guns for game big enough or crooked enough to deserve it. And even he can be beaten. H. R. Haldeman, former President Nixon's adviser, not only beat Mike Wallace; he got paid $50,000 for the pleasure. The wonder is that Mike Wallace didn't know any better after so many years of playing the game for CBS News. Haldeman worked Wallace like a bullfighter. He volunteered no information; he simply answered the questions as succinctly and superficially as possible. He never lost his temper, while Wallace, ever more angry, began to badger Haldeman ever more intensely. Wallace charged in with one loaded question after another, while Haldeman skirted his answers with a smile. The more accusatory the question, the softer the answer. Before long, the audience at home began rooting for Haldeman against his rude, insistent adversary.

Another characteristic of Mike Wallace's—his insistence on having answers repeated for ironic emphasis—added to the inquisitorial atmosphere. In one exchange,* Wallace asked whether President Nixon and Secretary of State Kissinger had any disagreement over the carpet-bombing of North Vietnam in December of 1971.

"Absolutely not," Haldeman said.

"None?" Wallace asked again.

"No," Haldeman repeated.

Quotable quotes.

"You *loved* Richard Nixon, didn't you?" Wallace asked.

"No, I didn't—and I don't," Haldeman answered rather emphatically.

*Copyright CBS Inc. 1975. All rights reserved. Originally broadcast March 23, 1975, and March 30, 1975, over the CBS Television Network, entitled "Haldeman: The Nixon Years."

"I'm not sure I understand," Wallace said, aiming for something better.

"It's a very concise answer," Haldeman said.

And so it was.

Haldeman's technique worked beautifully for an interviewee who never really wanted to say anything anyhow, but that approach won't do for someone who is trying to get a point across.

Interviewers who adopt a variation of the Mike Wallace attack usually have good reason to do so. By the time a news broadcaster gets a measure of reputation, he or she has been told more lies than an IRS agent. Sometimes they are bold, black lies; sometimes subtle half-truths:

The Acme Widget Company invites you to meet the president of AWC at 10 A.M. Monday morning in the executive offices of the company, where he will make a major announcement of a new research development that will have a vast impact on automobile gas mileage.

Taking no chances, all three networks, the wire services, fourteen major newspapers, three news-magazines, and all local stations and newspapers in a 100-mile radius show up at Acme headquarters, ready to transmit this great and far-reaching announcement to an eager public. At the appointed hour the president of Acme Widget unveils a new device that new car buyers can buy as an option to next year's models by two of the top three automakers. This option, a microprocessor-run display gizmo, tells you exactly how your gas mileage varies at different speeds and driving conditions. You don't get any more miles per gallon, you simply know how few—or many—you're getting.

Politicians are probably the best at this ploy. Every candidate in every presidential campaign has a major announcement at every airport landing. More often than not, the announcement is little more than a vaguely worded rehash of the story already in print in the morning newspapers followed by a five-minute dissertation on how happy the candidate is to be in (he turns to his press aide for a hurried conversation) "the great city of Springfield," he finishes triumphantly.

Couple dozens of repetitions of that experience with the silly evasions and gross overstatements of PR people, authors, and publishers, and you can understand reporters' cynicism. An interviewer who hears an author say, "I demonstrate in my book conclusively that hypnotism should replace psychiatry," has some reason for skepticism.

It is true that most interviewers treat a new guest with a measure of distance, but that is a direct result of having been burned so many times. The interviewer will look for that ulterior motive, that half-truth, that slip of the tongue that reveals a person's "real" reason for asking to be on the show. But if there are no hidden motives, no intent to deceive, no selfish reason disguised as altruism for the guest's visit, he or she has little to worry about, even if a confrontation develops.

Confrontations make exciting listening and viewing, and most of us believe, at least subconsciously, that truth will emerge when arguments and ideas are under attack. It's the public that favors debates between candidates, not necessarily the principals. The only problem is that confrontation does not always produce the naked truth. Look at what happened in the Wallace-Haldeman debates.

The most capable interviewers know that confrontation is at best a two-edged sword and therefore try to avoid it. People who relish confrontation can be beaten by an experienced interviewee, and one of the purposes of this book is to make more of those confrontations fair fights. If you go on a show trying to hide something, chances are the interviewer will discover that. If you don't really know what you are talking about, a good interviewer will make that clear, too. But if you meet the interviewer half way and know your stuff, the host will treat you like a guest.

If you meet one of those Neanderthal interviewers whose specialty is humiliation, take a lesson from H. R. Haldeman. Don't get into a brawl, but show some quiet indignation at your treatment without losing your temper. If the viewers could feel sorry for Haldeman, imagine how they'll feel toward you.

CHAPTER 8

PRACTICE MAKES PERFECT

Before the state grants you a driver's license, it asks you to familiarize yourself with the rules of the road and to pass a driving test, proving your competence behind the wheel. Getting ready to join the talk-show circuit, even on the smallest scale, demands a crash course in the rules of the airways.

One of the ways to learn is by listening to and watching every talk show you can. As you listen and watch, play different roles. Be the host, be the guest. Be a panelist asking questions on one of the network news interview shows. Get a feeling for the rhythm of a talk show, for how much can be said in a half hour.

When you're playing the guest, actually try to

answer the host's question, in the sense of how you would answer it in your own situation. Thus, when the host asks a guest to explain the history of an organization in a brief, informative way, do the same for your group. Note how questions tend to be repeated from show to show, starting from "establishing" questions (those that elicit the information from a guest that tells the audience who he or she is, what they have come to talk about), to questions that move the show from subject to subject. If there are three panelists and a host on a half hour show, the maximum amount of time you will have to talk is only about eight minutes, unless you hog the microphone. In eight minutes, especially when you must answer questions posed by the host, how can you get your point across? What is the simplest form of the message you need to deliver?

Don't just watch the talk shows. Watch televised press conferences, the interviews on regular news shows. If you have never been on radio or television before, make up a set of questions and answer them in the microphone of a tape recorder. Listen to your voice. It sounds funny at first, but how funny? Do you say "you know" after every third word? Do you mumble or hesitate or say "uh" a lot? Is your voice clear and steady, your enunciation crisp? If you hear a continuing series of crutch words or sounds, practice talking without them ("ya know" is probably the most prevalent crutch phrase these days). Then get a friend to ask you questions, to jump in and make you follow up on points. Put a time limit on it, so you are forced to think on your feet. After four or five sessions you'll see improvement and hear confidence in your responses. It's really a lot like learning to drive.

Over the next few years, as videocassette record-ers with camera attachments reach more and more American homes and businesses, it will be possible for more and more people to practice appearing before a camera, as well as a microphone. If you have access to such equipment now, make use of it. Have one friend act as cameraman and another as interviewer. Videotape a practice run and see how you look. Seeing yourself can be as helpful as hearing yourself, especially if you add the camera after you have become comfortable talking into the tape recorder. Make the situation as real as possible. Set strict time limits, allow for commercial breaks, make sure your "host" asks the embarrassing as well as the easy questions, and consider the job well done if you get butterflies in your stomach during the show.

CHAPTER 9

BEFORE

You're on the air from the moment you reach the station's entrance door. At least that's the only safe approach to make. This means you don't indulge in nervous gossipy chatter with anyone before the show, even an aide or a close friend who has come along to provide support.

"I tell you, Sid, I just don't understand how the FDA can even be considering a health warning on our inhaler. You don't suppose the guy on this show has gotten wind of that yet, do you?"

"I doubt it, Dave. We just got the first notice from the FDA yesterday. We'll probably go to court over it eventually."

"I'm sure glad there's no way a question like that will come up. It's hard as hell to explain how the fluorocarbon aerosol sneaked past us after the ban. Maybe he won't know about that either."

While Sid and Dave are bemoaning their latest tribulations, that harmless young woman who has been sent to the reception desk to fetch them is implanting every word in her tape-recorder mind. She's a trainee, working her way up, and a piece of grist like this could rush the day she becomes an assistant producer.

"Omigod, Dave, I sure hope he doesn't connect that explosion at our baby formula subsidiary with us. Most people don't realize we bought it last year, and that explosion put six people in the hospital."

TV and radio stations are full of people who want to become broadcast personalities or producers. See that distracted, daydreaming usher standing in the lobby? Not only does he have the ears of a piano tuner, but he also has a recent bachelor's degree in television, and he would sign away his soul for a chance to be on the air. To do that, he needs to be noticed favorably—and often—by the host or a producer.

The moment you're out of sight, he is sprinting off to relay that explosive information where it will do the most good *for him*.

That's one good argument for throwing away the crutch of a friend to hold your hand, or the comforting phalanx of staffers often favored by celebrities and chief executive officers. A retinue can get in your way—or worse, get in the station's way, especially if it's unexpected. Come alone if you can.

Do you know where you're going? Ever since the troubled 1960s, broadcasting stations have taken on the air of a fortress, especially at night. Be sure you know whom to ask for and which entrance to use. Nothing can irritate a host more than a guest who shows up late because he hasn't followed instructions. Seemingly minor lapses like this can cause a major backlash when the interview actually begins.

The best guests are just that. They have enough interest in the host and program to have watched it, or listened to it, beforehand. Professional interviewees, like book authors on cross-country tours, often have a rundown on the show from the publicity staff at home base. Sometimes they get information by calling the local paper's TV and radio critic, something any guest can do for himself. What kind of person is the host: A social activist? Well educated? A smart aleck? In love with controversy for its own sake? The kind who never reads the author's book (or does any homework)? The kind who knows more about the subject than the interviewee does? Is the person trained in journalism, or a recycled disk jockey? All that information helps.

Knowing the format of the show also helps, because it gives a guest a chance to anticipate the possible approaches the host may take to the interview, and it allows a guest to turn the conversation to the points he or she wants to make before the show runs out. If, for example, you know that this particular talk show moves to news or ends at five minutes to the hour, or the host cuts it off at 10 minutes to the hour in order to talk about the next show, you won't be waiting patiently for the host to get to your side of it at a quarter to the hour.

Knowing the host's biases and foibles may be even more important. If he is the kind that prepares for an interview like a Ph.D. candidate getting ready for his orals, that means you have to do the same. On the other hand, if the host's intellectual capability is on the level of a small bird, it may be possible to dazzle him or her with knowledge and take over the show.

One short-lived talk-show host was killed by the simplest appraisal of her show. Someone who asked what sort of interviewer she was got for an answer the story of the time she interviewed a cancer researcher. "Tell me, Dr. X," the interviewer asked blandly, "what causes cancer anyhow?" Armed with that story, guest after guest took over the show, until station management wised up and got a new host.

You may be able to find out a great deal about the host's *past* performance, but your chances of getting advance information on your own upcoming interview depend a lot on the impression you make on the host before the show. With rare exceptions, they aren't fools, so don't gush. When you meet the host or the producer, don't blather on ad nauseam about how "honored" or "flattered" you are to be there, unless you really mean it. It's okay to tell Johnny Carson how influential he is and how much it means to you to talk to his huge audience, but don't try that one on the host of a radio talk show that goes on the air at 1 A.M.

A polite, nondemanding request that the host tell you what he hopes to cover in the interview is fine. The host is not omniscient, and unless you tell him what you would like to talk about in the interview, he may never get around to asking the right questions. Asking the host what *he* wants to cover also permits you to explain clearly what *you* want to talk about. "As consumer affairs director of the company, I can't explain exactly how our new technical process works, but I *can* explain the impact of this process on consumers. We're anxious to let consumers know what benefits they'll have from this, and from some other things we're doing too, so if we could get into our new service program and the changes in our warranties sometime during the interview, I'd be grateful."

Now the host knows what you know, what you don't, and what you are prepared to talk about.

If you're invited to the show to argue against paving over the only park in forty blocks and you can't make heads or tails of a park district budget, say so. "Look, the reason I'm involved in S.O.P. (Save Our Park) is because of the kids. If that park becomes a parking lot, there just won't be any place left for them to play, and with the growing amount of delinquency in the city, we need every place for kids we can get. Now *that* I know about, and I have the figures to support it."

And you'd better have those figures on paper. Notes are a professional touch. You don't see your income tax preparer without them, and you don't go to an important business meeting without notes, do you? This doesn't mean that you write out answers on 3-by-5 cards and *read* the "acceptable" answer to a sticky question the S.O.B. was sure to ask. But it helps keep your statistics straight and your credibility intact. It's O.K. to read a couple of sentences from a policy statement, but don't bring a whole fifty-page report and attempt to read it unless you intend to drive the entire audience to their "off" buttons.

Be honest. If the host is determined to draw and quarter you, there isn't much you can do to stop the dreaded questions. But if you throw yourself on his or her mercy, you just might get compassionate co-operation. One reason you may need help is a nasty

47

situation over which you, your company, or your organization has no control. Because it has been in the news, you can be quite sure the host has heard of it. But if you really can't say anything cogent about it, bring it up with the host before the show begins: "Bob, as you're probably aware, the brother of our president had two paternity suits filed against him last week. I don't know any more about it than what's been in the news. I'd appreciate it if it didn't come up in the interview, but if it does, that's all I can say about it." Then hope for the best.

The larger the organization, the more likely it is that someone other than the actual guest will make the approach to the show's host or producer. Some public relations people, thinking they are being helpful, try to make demands on the show in exchange for the appearance. Some want to review the questions and approve them in advance. Others want to dictate a list of subjects pleasing to the guest. Still others want veto power over other guests on the show. All of them are overstepping their rights, and building resentment on the host's part against a guest who may know nothing about these plans.

Although it is fine for you to take control of a show once the cameras are on, don't approach the show as though you and your minions are staging a coup. The technique raises hostilities and will surely get you off to a bad start. If you are not making your own pitch to the show, make sure those who are doing so understand the ground rules.

When you are in the studio or meeting the host, don't demand to know exactly what will be covered in the ensuing interview. Even if the host is holding notes with typed or written questions, don't ask to see them. They are the host's notes, just as your notes are your personal and private property. The host reserves the right to depart from prepared questions, just as the guest does, and pressing the host for a peek only insures a fast and perhaps vicious attack on the guest. No matter how good you may be at counter-attacking, such exchanges will hurt you.

Just as a wise guest measures the content of remarks on the way into the studio, so must he also watch the quality of his language. Profanity or vulgarity in the studio will lead to disaster. It may be tempting to match four letters with four letters as a way of ingratiating yourself with the host or the crew, but it's too risky. Even though the show is not yet on the air, what goes into live microphones can be taped by the engineers. And there are engineers from coast to coast and across the fruited plains who gleefully and voraciously collect the gutter language of the famous and the vulgarities of the masses to trade, share, and sell among friends. These are *permanent* transcriptions, remember, and the value of the filth on the open market is in direct proportion to the rank and prestige of the speaker.

Today you may be promoting a stoplight at a busy intersection, but when you run for mayor ten years from now those tapes may be your downfall.

A TV APPEARANCE THAT LOST AN ELECTION

If it weren't for television, Charles Percy probably would not be senator from Illinois. In 1978, when Senator Percy was running for his third term in the Senate, his Democratic challenger was a relative unknown in Illinois named Alex Seith. Percy, who figured, along with most observers, that he had the election locked up, did very little early campaigning in the state.

Seith, determined to win, hired media whiz Tony Schwartz from New York to do his broadcast campaign. On some radio stations there were "candid interviews" with "voters" complaining about the absentee senator. Similar versions appeared on television with carefully selected "voters" complaining that Senator Percy's opinions on issues changed with each audience, and so forth. And on black radio stations there was a special campaign featuring an ad that quoted Percy as saying he wished Earl Butz was secretary of agriculture again. Because Butz had been in trouble with some racist jokes made public by John Dean, the implication of the ad was that Senator Percy was a closet racist. The campaign went downhill from there, and less than a week before the election Percy was as much as 17 percent behind Seith in the polls.

Then on Friday afternoon, November 3, 1978, four days before the election, it was time to tape a Sunday morning local news show to be broadcast right before the Bears football game on the Sunday before election. The show, *Newsmakers,* is a regular program on the CBS station in Chicago, and Walter Jacobson, the station's political pundit and co-anchor of the evening news, was the moderator. The scheduled guests: Charles Percy and Alex Seith.

That morning the Chicago newspapers carried a Percy campaign ad. It was a reprint of an anti-Seith column written by Mike Royko. The column dealt with a court case in which Seith had testified as a character witness for a man whose relatives had unsavory connections with the mob, which Royko duly spelled out. Moreover, the man worked for Seith in a government agency, and Royko called Seith to task for testifying on behalf of a man indicted for bribery. But the headline laid on top of the column was indicative of the state of the campaign. It read, "Pulitzer Prize Winner Mike Royko" (in big type), and in smaller type: "Tells more about the mob, the Chicago machine, and Alex Seith."

51

The guilt-by-association in that headline was quite a bit stronger than the story underneath it, and Seith was frantic. He showed up at the station considerably in advance of the taping deadline and camped out in the lobby, waiting to confront Percy about the ad. Now it is customary at this station to get shots of newsmakers in the building to use as lead-ins for excerpts from the taped show (if it turns out to be newsworthy) to be run as a feature on the regular 10 P.M. news. So a camera crew was dispatched to the lobby to get some shots of a steaming Seith. By design or accident, Percy entered the building through a side door, and sure enough, a camera crew was there to get some footage of the senator striding off to the makeup room.

Having missed that chance, Seith went up to the *Newsmakers* set and sat with host Walter Jacobson to wait for Percy. The technicians swarmed around, fitting microphones, adjusting lights, and so forth. A videotape camera was running. The studio was filled with all manner of reporters, Seith's campaign staff—and his wife. The camera was running, the lights were on, and the tape duly recorded all that happened. As Seith and Jacobson settled themselves in their chairs, Seith said, "I'm not making any physical contact with him, not even shaking hands. I'll say what I want to say and not make physical contact."

The set is a platform, with three chairs and a phony window backdrop, and Mrs. Seith and a campaign aide took seats a step or two to the side of the platform.

Just then, one of Seith's aides walked up on the set and whispered in his ear. Later Jacobson reported that the aide had told Seith to shake hands with Percy if he walked onto the set. And sure enough, when the Senator appeared, Seith gave him a warm handshake, despite his earlier angry joke that someone (meaning one of the nearby reporters) might make something of it if he clasped Percy's hand too hard.

But before Percy could be miked and settled, Seith motioned his wife up onto the platform and asked Percy to explain the offending headline in front of his wife. In machine-gun fashion he asked Percy why he wrote the headline, whether he thought Seith really was part of the mob, and whether he'd checked with his libel lawyers. Mrs. Seith stood there and cried. From several remarks he made, Seith indicated that he knew the cameras were running. Percy, however, did not seem to be aware that the cameras were running. Percy asked Seith to hold his remarks and discuss the matter "publicly," meaning on the show, for of course the reporters were madly taking notes.

Finally, Jacobson asked Mrs. Seith to leave the set, and the show's official taping began. It was not politics' finest hour. Seith baited Percy, and Percy began slugging on the same level, albeit with temper mostly in check. A half hour of charges and countercharges later, the show ended, but the argument didn't.

The two men parted bitterly, and Percy walked out into the hallway to face all the reporters, cameras, and lights waiting out there. He apologized for the headline, reiterated that he had not seen it before it had gone into the paper, and promised to remove it from all the other editions and newspapers scheduled to carry the ad before the election Tuesday.

Then he fainted.

And it was the faint that set everything in motion. (True to form, after the election, at least one high-ranking Democrat accused Percy of faking it.) Percy was only down for a moment—he attributed it to the press of bodies and the heat of the lights—but anyone who has ever been in a tight public battle like that can appreciate the strain on the senator. It is also possible that the senator had a delayed, intense case of nerves after the unexpected combat.

The WBBM-TV management huddled, and by 10 P.M. reached a decision. The entire episode, from the first shot of Seith in the lobby to Senator Percy's faint, uncut and unedited, would be shown at the conclusion of the evening news that night. At 10:15, mid-news, the station had a 17.9 rating; by 10:30 it had gone over 18 (and at one point the Seith-Percy drama had a rating higher than the network prime-time offering that preceded the news). Even at 11:45, when the show ended, the rating was still 13. In contrast, Johnny Carson's *Tonight Show* on NBC and the 10:30 P.M. offering at the ABC station each had a rating of 8.

Walter Jacobson delivered a commentary during the broadcast, even in the spots reserved for the commercials that would run with the official show on Sunday. After the studio tape ended, Minicam crews followed the two candidates through their evening's campaign stops.

Those viewers who saw only the show on Sunday, and many did, may have thought both candidates came off badly, but their friends who saw the Friday night version set them straight. Percy won the election handily.

That impromptu, technically terrible, Friday night show was quite simply some of the most exciting television Chicagoans had seen in years. The gloves-off, masks-off confrontation between the candidates was about as close a look as voters will ever get of the true character of political opponents in an election. They saw Seith being wishywashy about the handshaking. They saw Percy holding his temper, arguing his side, but admitting he was wrong when he saw the light, and they saw the toll of his ordeal when he fainted. Instead of working to Seith's advantage, the whole episode backfired. Instead of his wife's tears generating sympathy for him, her appearance made him look like a man without the courage to fight his own battles. As those cameras ground on, his lead dissipated before everyone's eyes.

The contrast of the gracious loser who conceded defeat on Tuesday with the conniving, ambitious candidate who provoked a confrontation on Friday was an expensive lesson for Alex Seith, but it is a lesson many can profit from. Those who seek to manipulate the media may find themselves media victims. Seith, no doubt, hoped to provoke Percy into a mistake, hoped that snippets of that pre-show badinage would make the evening news, present him as a honest man wronged. Instead, it made him look like a hypocrite. Too bad this time, but in his next race for senator in 1980, Alex Seith avoided those mistakes. Instead, he produced a TV documentary and bought time on stations throughout the state to show it. Unfortunately for him, a popular opponent and low ratings for his show added up to a defeat in the primaries.

You can use the media, but it can use you, too. Even a small show (*Newsmakers* is not a very popular Sunday morning show) can do you in or make you.

CHAPTER 11

COSMETICS

Network shows and the larger stations in major cities always have someone on hand to help a guest with makeup. Others do not, so it is best to assume that no makeup will be available in most small stations. TV makeup, unlike stage or street makeup, is not intended to create a character or a dramatic look for a face. It has a very practical purpose: it prevents the strong studio lights from using your face as a reflector beacon. Without makeup, the lights have a tendency to bounce off a face with an unpleasant shine. A touch of pancake, however, lets your face absorb the light, giving you a smoother, more natural look.

If you ordinarily wear pancake makeup, just put it on carefully, and if you don't wear it, screw up your courage and ask for help at a cosmetics counter. Ask for a pancake makeup to suit your coloring. Testing it on the back of the hand is standard procedure. Look for a color as close to your own skin color as possible, cheating toward a slightly darker shade if you can't get an exact match. Buy an applicator sponge, too, and some cream or lotion for removing makeup.

Then practice at home, whether or not you ordinarily wear makeup. If you are lucky enough to have access to a videotape camera for rehearsal, by all means wear your makeup for that. Dab on a light coat, covering all the exposed skin. Many people make the mistake of putting on too much makeup, which is as bad as no makeup at all, because your skin takes on a chalky, one-color effect that looks very artificial. If you can see no gradation in your skin tone after applying the makeup, you have too much on.

If the top of your head is bald, cover it all. If your hairline is receding, make sure you get the makeup *into* the hairline, not just across the middle of the forehead. If you can manage it without slopping it all over your shirt, get it down to the collar on your neck. If you can't do that, blend it under your jaw so that there is no line of demarkation. Women should carry the makeup down under the neckline of the dress or suit. A partial makeup job can be worse than no makeup at all, because you'll look as if you have a mask on.

Whatever the fashion on the street, women should beware of the bold rouged look. Simply wear enough blusher to give a slightly rosy tone across the cheekbones, and make sure that it blends imperceptibly into the cheek near the hairline. Lipstick should not be a vivid shade of red, but one of the muted, dusty tones. Don't wear lip gloss. Instead, if you wish, finish your lips with a dusting of powder, and make sure you have applied and blotted enough layers of lipstick to last throughout the show. If you can't be sure, you'd be wise to forgo all but the most minimal lip treatment.

Eyelashes, if false, should look real. If you can put your face four inches from an illuminated makeup mirror without destroying the illusion, your eyelashes are O.K. The same goes for mascara. No lumps, no noticeable stiffness from four inches.

Women who are very skillful with makeup may wish to sculpt their faces subtly for the camera. A layer of light-colored blemish eraser applied sparingly below the eye will mask bags and wrinkles—but just to the bottom edge of the eyesocket, please. Eyeshadow should be equally light, almost imperceptible, with a light color under the brows, a darker brown, mauve, or other neutral color on the lids. To thin the face, suck in your cheeks and apply a tiny bit of taupe or mauve eye shadow in the hollow, blending it to near invisibility. This accents the cheekbones and minimizes the jaw. Finally, apply a little blush-on down the ridge of your nose and on the tip of your chin. When you're through, only the differences should be visible, not the cosmetics used to achieve them.

Makeup can have another benefit, too. If you are a person who perspires easily, a filmy layer of makeup will help close your pores and reduce the amount of visible perspiration.

If you apply the pancake evenly, makeup cannot hurt you; the lack of makeup may indeed hurt a performance. The televised campaign debates in

1960 between John F. Kennedy and Richard Nixon
are historic by now.

The first was scheduled for Chicago. Kennedy
arrived rested and tanned from California, and he
wore no makeup. He would have worn it, had he not
been tanned. Nixon at that time was not very
knowledgeable about television, and he decided
against cosmetics entirely, save for a little shave
stick. On the way into the studio, he bashed his knee
on a car door and was in some pain, which was an
unfortunate handicap to compound the usual distress
of appearing before cameras.

Nixon decided against makeup because he
thought Kennedy or the press or the public would
make fun of him for using it. Shortly into the debate,
he began to perspire visibly, right through his shave
stick. Kennedy, who in addition to his tan had very
lucky sweat glands, stayed dry.

After the debate, national polls showed something
very curious. Those who watched the debate on
television thought Kennedy had won. Those who
listened on radio thought Nixon had won. Nixon
concentrated on substance and addressed the
issues. Kennedy addressed the people and relied on
style. But more people watched the debate on TV
than listened on radio. Q.E.D., style won.

Had Nixon used makeup for that appearance,
things might have been a little different.

Finally, if you do not ordinarily wear makeup,
remember to remove it before you see anyone after
the broadcast. Although some TV makeup comes off
with soap and water alone, usually removal cream
and a box of tissues are required. You will need to
wash the residue of the cream off your face. Most
people look askance at a man in makeup who is not
on a stage. Why present the temptation?

CHAPTER 12

WARDROBE

When you go on television, you are selling yourself and perhaps your ideas, not your excellent judgment in fashion. Don't wear anything so flashy that it draws attention away from you to your packaging.

Despite technical advances, avoid white. White shirts and blouses still flare in the lights occasionally, and light blue fades out in a Chromakey rear projection. Gray, darker blues, yellows, and beiges are much better choices for the camera. Black is also to be avoided, because it absorbs too much light. Men should be sure to wear long, knee-high socks. No exceptions. And they should be darker than the suit.

Always keep a double-breasted jacket buttoned. You may unbutton a single-breasted coat, but you should keep it fairly well in front of you. Never let it flop open too wide.

Wear only one patterned item, and make sure it's a quiet pattern. If your tie is patterned, wear a solid shirt and preferably a solid suit. Avoid herringbone and similar designs. They have a tendency to "crawl" on television, an optical effect that makes the pattern look as if it is strangely animated.

The rules against busy-looking clothing apply to women, too, but their problems are more complex. Find out what color the set is. One guest on the *Today* show planned to wear a snappy designer suit in bright red for her appearance. The set was bright orange. You are always safe with neutral colors— navy, varying shades of gray, brown, or khaki.

Try to avoid wearing something new, but if you must, test it first by sitting in a chair in front of a mirror. Does it add forty pounds when you sit down? Is your skirt long enough to keep you modest, no matter how heated the discussion? Try the chair trick with an older outfit, too. Occasionally what you feel comfortable in looks terrible, but being in a familiar dress, suit, or pantsuit relieves some of the burden of the experience. It's one less thing to worry about.

Prints with a pattern that includes flowers, geometric forms, animals, or other recognizable objects in a size larger than an inch square are best avoided. Viewers will watch the dress instead of you.

And unless your TV appearance is meant to get you a part in a porno flick, don't wear anything see-through, avoid the nippled look, and shun any neckline that shows cleavage unless it can be completely masked by a securely tied and anchored scarf.

Don't overdress or underdress. Clothing you would expect to see on a bank vice president will do you at any hour. Men should get no more casual than a sport jacket in lieu of a suit. Women, while they need not wear a formal suit of the sort John T. Molloy recommends for successful dress, should wear a skirt rather than a pantsuit if they are not of perfect figure. The skirt may be a suit with jacket or a dress, but it should fall in that same range of muted colors mentioned above. If it's an evening show, a long skirt and sweater or tailored jacket are fine. In the afternoon, a long skirt looks out of place—people will think you're on the way to a cocktail party.

A word about jewelry. Wedding rings and watches are fine, but anything else requires close scrutiny. Jangly bracelets are out, and chains or necklaces are appropriate only if the wearer is sure they will not clunk against a lavaliere microphone or make any sort of independent noise a microphone might pick up. Be prepared to take off at the last moment any jewelry that might interfere.

Eyeglasses: if you wear them ordinarily, wear them on television. Try not to wear chrome or shiny metal frames, because they can catch light and flare. To be especially secure, move the bows slightly up off your ears (provided you have hair to cover them). This angles the lenses down slightly as insurance against glare from the lights on the set. The best frames? Tortoise shell.

CHAPTER 13

LITTLE THINGS MEAN A LOT

Plant your rear solidly in the chair. Exactly where you plant it depends on the kind of chair it is and the kind of person you are. If you spend most of your day at a desk, sit in the chair as you would sit at your desk. Whatever position you pick, make sure you are sitting erect, with as few folds around your middle as possible. If you are in a swivel chair, you will want to swing it into a desired position and then plant yourself in it. Place your feet firmly on the floor to keep the chair stationary.

Sitting erect will leave your chest cavity free and uncompressed, so that you can speak without running out of breath. You need not sit all the way back in the chair, or even parallel with the back. It may be more comfortable for you to sit at an angle, toward the host, with your forearm resting on the arm of the chair or along the back of it. (On a radio show, you will want to sit erect, but your comfort must be in relation to the microphone, not the host.)

It's good to cross your legs. Crossed legs, or at least crossed ankles, give a neater and more relaxed look. But do not recline or slouch in order to cross your legs, or for any other reason.

If you sit at an angle, you will have one hand occupied. If you do not, you need to find something to do with your hands. If the seating arrangement allows a table or lectern in front of you, treat it as you would a desk top and use it as a hand rack. You can rest your hands in your lap, folded or unfolded. You can use your hands to hold something—note cards, a manila folder, or an envelope. Even if you intend to use no notes, it's not a bad idea to carry blank cards or other papers as a prop, just to keep your hands out of harm's way.

Some people are very good with their hands. They can place one hand lightly against their chin while another panelist or the host is talking, or sit with one arm crossed and the other over the mouth and chin in a position of thoughtful attention. But they remember to *remove their hands from their faces* when it is their turn to talk. If there is even a vague chance that you will forget to take your hand down when it's your turn to respond, train yourself to keep your hands below the level of your chest. This is particularly important if you have a nervous habit involving anything above your chin—rubbing your head (or eye, nose, ear, or chin), twisting your hair, tapping a fingernail against a tooth, or some other distracting gesture. If you aren't aware of having such a habit, ask someone who knows you well and who will tell you the truth. Your family or friends will have noticed it. Once you are conscious of a habit, practice doing something else, or at least being aware of when and how you do it. With deliberate effort you will be able to stop.

If you gesture naturally when you talk, do so on the interview. If you don't, don't suddenly introduce gestures for the camera.

It might seem simple just to cross your arms for the duration of the show, but it's a bad idea for more than a few minutes when you don't have the floor. Crossed arms tend to hunch the body over and compress the chest, leaving you breathless when an unexpected question comes your way. Whatever position you choose, it should provide enough leverage for you to lean forward at will.

Under ordinary circumstances, it looks bad to touch the host or another panelist as you talk. It can make you look sniveling, as if you are begging for attention. But used sparingly, it can be a good tool when the going gets rough. You may have to contend with a rude guest or an overly loquacious host who doesn't give you time to finish your thoughts. When the situation becomes intolerable, it can be very effective to lean forward suddenly and place a firm hand on the host's arm (sometimes even the leg). Almost invariably that sudden movement will make a speaker pause, and that's your entry. (A movement upward is equally effective.)

Whatever you bring for notes or as a prop for your hands, don't hide it. You need something big enough for the audience to see (not Captain Queeg's steel balls). Moreover it must be something you can hold easily in one hand in case the other is needed to shake hands or create some interruption ploy. It can be as small as a pen, or as big as a book or a legal pad.

If you suddenly get a frog in your throat or an intense need to cough, don't fight it. Resolve it. It happens to everybody. Simply turn away from the microphone, whether on television or radio, and cough or clear your throat. You're not in a sanctuary and there is no reason to strangle.

Always assume that your face—and your entire body, for that matter—is on the viewing screen. Do so regardless of what is happening on the show, even during the host's opening introduction. This is no problem when you are doing the talking, but when you're not talking, keep in mind that whatever you do can be seen. Reaction shots make wonderful television, so stay alert. If you tense up, primp, look dartingly around the studio as if for escape, yawn, mop your brow, or do anything else that might be misinterpreted by the audience at home, chances are it will be.

The original Kennedy-Nixon debates are an object lesson on reaction shots. Whatever ground Nixon didn't lose through the lack of makeup, he lost through the reaction shots, because the audience had a chance to watch him sweat silently, while they listened to Kennedy's measured cadences. In that Chicago debate, which was directed by Don Hewitt (who went on to produce *60 Minutes*), staffers on both sides actually counted reaction shots and requested equal numbers as the show progressed. The damage such shots can do has become so well understood that ground rules for the 1976 debates between Jimmy Carter and Gerald Ford forbade reaction shots of either the debaters or the audience.

CHAPTER 14

BE YOURSELF

Those who knew him well insist that Lyndon Johnson, in small private conferences, was one of the most expressive and dynamic communicators who ever occupied the White House. Quick-witted and earthy, Johnson also kidded people unmercifully—including himself, they said. But when Johnson went on television, he sounded like the narrator of a third-rate historical pageant. If his style in public was the result of some "expert" advice, the expert should have gone on the Republican payroll.

Lyndon Johnson was not being himself.

Silly as it sounds, many people who are guests on television and radio shows try to play-act. Usually the

role is overly reserved, pseudodignified, and pomp-
ous, the role Johnson affected. Maybe it's the
unfamiliarity of the situation, maybe it's just plain
stagefright. Whatever the cause, the result is the
same: the audience perceives the person as a phony,
a boob, or even worse—a liar.

You do yourself a great disservice if you succumb
to the temptation to try out for some imagined role of
statesman-saint or hail-fellow-well-met or stand-up
comedian. The people at home tune in just as much
to get acquainted with the *real* you as to hear you
expound on your ideas. Be honest. Let your personality be seen (unless one of your traits is to fly into a
rage whenever someone contradicts you). If someone
asks a preposterous question, laugh out loud if it
strikes you funny. Don't retreat into some amateur
personality adopted for the occasion.

"When you musicians aren't getting blasted on
some controlled substance, what do you do in your
off-hours?" If you look too passive after a question
like that, half the people tuning in will think the
interviewer is really on to something.

Remember, you're a guest in the viewers' home.
Let the occupants get to know you. If you have a
good sense of humor, use it—or a strong vocabulary
(within bounds of good taste), or an analytical mind,
or a sense of mission about your case, or whatever
else your friends would recognize as *you.* Be
yourself.

That advice applies to broadcasters, too. There
are a few people in the broadcast business who
could use this advice at least as much as guests.
Some of them are the bush-league newscasters who
try to adopt the deliberate cadences of a David
Brinkley, unsuccessfully. Or the broadcasters who

lower their natural speaking voice an octave (a favorite ploy decades ago in radio). They end up looking ridiculous, as does a normally serious person who suddenly tries to be funny in honor of the occasion, or a physically reserved guest who suddenly adds gestures to his or her conversation.

All of us have our own strengths. Use *them,* not somebody else's.

CHAPTER 15

THE AWFUL (WONDERFUL) EXPERIENCE

So there you are with lights slowly frying the top of your head and a microphone clipped to your clothes or hanging around your neck or looming over your head like some great bird beak ready to peck you silly if you make a mistake—and the show is on.

How do you know the show is on? The little red tally light on the camera is glowing like a stoplight. Sally Quinn, briefly co-host of the CBS *Morning News* with Hughes Rudd, claims she never knew about that little red light until it was too late, but she must be the only television person in the country kept in ignorance. The little red light tells you which camera is on, and usually you can see it easily out of the corner of your eye at least part of the time the show is being broadcast or taped.

From the time the first little red light goes on until the last little red light blinks off at the end of a show, something nice is going to happen: whatever outrageous requests were made of you before the show began in terms of the way you sit or pitch your voice, once the little red light goes on, you can sit and talk in whatever position or tone of voice you please. The engineers will have to compensate if your voice is too low or too loud, although that should have been settled before airtime with a voice level. Within reason, the same applies to the cameramen. They have to get a shot of your face; you don't have to look for the camera.

On the other hand, it helps to think of the camera in front of you as another person in the conversational circle. Just as you try to make eye contact with the person across from you in a conversational group, it's nice to glance at the camera lens now and again as if it were another person. Don't overdo it, and don't become a contortionist, but when the little red light catches your eye, glance its way. That's the audience out there, and that's who you really want to speak to anyhow. Really good television communicators all but invent a biography for that one-eyed person with the red light. And really good radio communicators, like Arthur Godfrey, use the microphone as they would use a telephone receiver with their best friend on the other end of the line.

There are not millions of people watching television through that Cyclopean eye, but one. How many people watch television in your house as a group? That's how many people are watching you. Think of yourself as an invited guest in someone's living room

"Polly, this is Agnes. We're asking all our friends to watch the eleven-o'clock news. Somebody stuck a mike in Bill's face to-day and asked him what he thought about something."

(or bedroom), politely waiting to give your opinion on a subject. The only difference is that you are sitting down in a large number of living rooms—one at a time. Picture just one, and talk to the occupants of that room. They're watching through the lens. And if you can glance at that lens as you would glance across a room, making eye contact with everyone present, you'll come across well. But if your eye contact with the lens has a mechanical checklist quality about it, you'll come off as a phony. If you can imagine the camera as a person, do so. If you can't, just relate to the host or the other guests and forget about the red lights.

Even if you aren't looking at the real people out there, think about them. It doesn't matter what the host or your fellow panelists think about you. It *does* matter what the audience thinks of you. The only exceptions to this might be the *Tonight Show* and the Phil Donahue show. If Johnny Carson is there and you annoy him, no matter how much the studio audience loves it, your cause is hurt. The people at home usually trust Carson's instincts too much to side with a guest against him. Donahue, too, receives tremendous loyalty from his audience. Although he encourages spirited discussion, his audience brooks very little rudeness either to Donahue himself or to his assistant hosts—the members of the studio audience who also ask questions.

Although your host may have done some homework to become familiar with your cause, it does not follow that the viewers have prepared to watch the program. They don't know the jargon of your profession or the intricacies of your organization, so don't cut them out. Why talk about a maldistribution of primary health-care deliverers, when you can just as easily talk about the shortage of family doctors in some areas of the country?

Bureaucratese and academese are out. It's grades, not performance evaluation. It's a shovel, not a portable, manually operated earth relocator. Jargon may have been invented as a shortcut to speed communication in a business or profession, but jargonese is designed to exclude the uninitiated. Maximize your input of clear colloquial English, and you'll minimize the downtime of sets tuned in.

This is not to suggest that you should patronize people or oversimplify your story. If a fancy word (in the English language, please, not jargonese) is best, use it. But the chances are that something simpler is just as good—and far more meaningful to the audience. William F. Buckley, for example, occasionally suffers from linguistic overkill. His operating vocabulary is larger than most people's, but too often he flaunts it to the detriment of the show. Don't follow that example.

All this advice is very good, but it assumes that you are in control of your endocrine system. The probability of that is so low as to be unmeasurable.

Degrees of terror are the natural state for a talk-show guest. As a rule when the studio hushes and the countdown begins: 10 seconds, 5 seconds . . . the guest's hands turn cold, clammy, almost numb. Some can feel sweat breaking out on their foreheads or under their arms. The heart pounds at the command of adrenalin until the guest swears the engineers must be able to hear it through the microphones. Hearing and vision seem to lose their acuity, and the body turns inward on itself. Breathing can become rapid and shallow, almost a pant. The mouth dries, and the guest in extremis may feel a need to run for the nearest bathroom. Leg and arm muscles tense. Left to run its course, this natural state can leave a guest feeling as if he or she has no control over what is about to happen. Some guests sit in a near trance, answering mechanically, but having no conception of what has been said once the show is over.

That reaction is called the fight-or-flight syndrome. You can thank your earliest ancestors for it, for whom it meant survival. What is happening is quite simple: the body is readying its physical capabilities for great exertion. You are either going to face this danger and fight to a conclusion, or you are going to turn tail and

run for safety as far and as fast as your legs will take
you. Fight-or-flight was not developed for a cerebral
civilization, but for a physical one. Unfortunately, the
body can't tell the difference between a mental threat
and a physical one. It hears only threat, turns on all
the switches of the endocrine system, and there you
are on the edge of gibbering idiocy.

The phenomenon is commonly known as stagefright, or "flop sweats," in a public performance
situation, although the symptoms are exactly the
same as those you develop after the car skids on an
icy road and you barely miss careening into the
opposite lane. A sense of danger brings it on, and
performing in public is perceived as dangerous by
almost everyone, even people who do it regularly for
a living.

A little bit of fight-or-flight is good. It makes you
alert, gives you that edge that helps you react faster,
think more clearly, perform at peak levels. But too
much is destructive. Unless you are superhuman, you
will not be able to escape the first stages, so the best
approach is to control the signs when first you notice
them, and to anticipate and eliminate, if possible, the
problems that could cause fight-or-flight. Being well
prepared helps, because you will perceive that your
"weapons" are ready. But if knowing you can handle
the questions doesn't allay the symptoms, at least try
to *look* calm. Sit still, and regulate your breathing.

Having no signs of fight-or-flight conversely is
bad. It may mean that you are bored with the
assignment, or that you belted down one too many
beforehand. What makes it truly dangerous is that the
full syndrome could come on you in mid-show,
making you look as if you had suffered instant
lobotomy.

Dealing with fight-or-flight takes practice, beginning with the conviction that a little nervousness is a good thing, not a sign of weakness. The next step is the acceptance of tension as a natural state in this situation. Some people—even professionals—never get over it. Richard Burton, after decades as an actor, still may tell an audience: "I feel as if every butterfly in the world has settled in my stomach." No two public performances are exactly the same, and that's why the syndrome continues.

It is not shameful to *look* nervous. On the contrary, the audience is likely to pull for someone who has turned to jelly before their eyes, regardless of what they think of the jellyfish's ideas. Besides, no matter how bad you *feel*, you never look bad. Tension must reach outrageous proportions before it shows visibly. Just about everyone rates him- or herself as more sweat-prone than the average, because we can never feel the *other* guy's heartbeat.

Two more comforting thoughts about discomfort:

You're not alone. A recent survey indicates that people in general are more terrified of appearing before an audience than they are of insects, darkness, heights, illness, or elevators.

There is a high probability that the *absence* of stagefright correlates with low intelligence. *Not* to worry about your performance, in other words, is just plain dumb.

CHAPTER 16

YOUR BILL OF RIGHTS

You may darken a studio door only once in your life, but you still have the right to be treated with courtesy and consideration, as outlined in these commandments of broadcast hospitality, written by a New York television director for guests on his show. (The italics are ours.)

1. A guest will be expected at the front door of the station at an appointed hour. The receptionist will be told. She, in turn, will call the producer or host when the guest arrives. The guest, in turn, will be escorted to the studio or green room by someone on the staff, perhaps even the producer or host.*

*So-called green rooms are places where guests wait to go on the air. They're universally called green rooms because the Tonight Show has a green room, adopted in turn from the green room in theaters where actors wait for entrance cues.

2. Once in the studio, the guest will be introduced by name to the floor director, who will immediately explain that most of his cues and signals during the show are intended for the host, not the guest. (Guests have no responsibility to help the staff with the production of the show, despite the fact that help is often needed.) The guest will then be escorted to his chair, rigged with a microphone, and looked at on-camera to be sure the lights are right. For those guests who want to look at themselves on-camera, the studio monitor will be pushed forward into plain sight. (It will also be pushed back before the show starts so the guest won't be tempted to peek at himself while we're on the air.)

3. After everything is correctly lighted and the other preliminaries are completed, the guest will be invited off the set so as not to fry him under the hot lights. If there is time, he will be offered a cup of coffee from the machine. (In the presence of the guest, the crew's and the staff's language will be that befitting a convention of Baptist ministers.)

4. Visual aids and props will be rehearsed. The director will not take kindly to being surprised by them once the show is on the air. If the guest has a little prop in his inside breast pocket, that tidbit of information will be elicited by the floor director beforehand and communicated to the control room. The guest will also be shown where and how to hold the prop—in front of his chest below his chin, or closely beside his head. The guest will be told that a prop held at arm's length on television usually results in a shot of his armpit on-camera, nothing more.

5. There will be no wise-cracking or laughing it up by the crew, particularly the crew with headsets. Guests are often paranoiac and invariably think the crew is laughing at them, which is hardly ever the

case. (Usually it's just the latest ethnic joke.) We won't be sullen either. Let's try for pleasant and helpful.

6. A few guests will be apathetic, some will be arrogant, most will be apprehensive, but all are unique. Eccentric requests by a guest will be channeled to the producer or director.

When these rights are violated, it is almost always due to thoughtlessness or shiftlessness rather than malice. The great enemy of most TV crews is boredom. They've done it all before a thousand times, and you're just one more torso being televised.

Although mistreatment is infrequent and seldom severe, why not be ready for the worst? Here's a true story that shows what we mean. A sound engineer one day decided (for reasons no one will ever know) to mike a four-person panel with a stationary boom microphone. After fussing with the controls for a while, he marched into the studio and told the people on each end of the long table that they would have to speak up *a lot louder,* because they were farther from the mike. Instead of saying "I'm sorry, I'm much more comfortable talking at this level, can't you compensate some other way?" both guests complied and screamed their way through the entire show.

And during the simulation of a television show in one of our courses, the floor director explained to one guest that since his four-legged chair leaned sharply backward and to the right, *he* would be required to lean sharply forward and to the left in compensation. One look at the screen and you would have thought the guest was suffering from an exotic spinal disorder. When the guest later objected, the bad chair was instead given to the host. At least *he* was being paid.

When your rights are violated, either object (nicely) or ignore it as best you can.

CHAPTER 17

KEEPING THE HOST HAPPY

Most interviewers, competent or not, will try to make their guests look good. The best ones will be well prepared and almost all will be nice. Only a handful are lying in wait to mug their guests.

Even if you know otherwise, assume that your host is well prepared, and do likewise. Here's how the best hosts do it:

Ultimately a good host wants to know enough about you or the issues you will be talking about to ask intelligent questions. He or she may ask you to provide a biography of yourself, any newspaper clippings you may have of print interviews with you, and perhaps even a short statement of your cause or issue in writing. If you are an author, the host will want a copy of your book before the interview. He will skim it, if he's good; if he's *very* good, he will read it. All these materials may suggest certain subjects that go beyond what you have given the host. Like anybody else, the good host will research those subjects in an encyclopedia or other books. A good host will spend at least as much time researching an interview as is spent on the air, and some will go even further.

If you prepare to meet this ideal host, you will be a match for the best.

Often a host will attempt to balance a show by providing two or more sides of a controversial question. The fact that the host has invited your nemesis on the show should not be a sign that he hates you, only that he or she is providing a forum for all sides. No matter how much you loathe the other panelists, keep your temper. Let them have their turns fairly. If you attempt a personal attack, you may be sorry, because hosts have a way of kicking unruly guests in the groin.

Don't hurt your cause by alienating the host. You have your hands full just getting your story across and politely countering your opposition. The host can tip the scale irreparably against you. Hosts appreciate fair fights, based on the issues. They take a dim view of personal attacks and bad manners. So does the audience, ultimately. Keep your temper and play by the rules.

Mohandas Gandhi said it best: "When you are in the right, you can afford to keep your temper. When you are in the wrong, you cannot afford to lose it."

CHAPTER 18

LISTENING

How well you hear is as important as how well you talk. The best interviewers are very good listeners. They don't always follow a prepared set of questions right down the line, but they listen to a guest's answer to one question and ask another that grows out of the answer. The best interviewees do the same thing. They listen to what the host says, as well as what the host asks; they listen to their fellow guests, too.

It's important to listen to *everything* that's said, because what you don't hear can hurt you. One of the facts of life in television and radio panel and discussion shows is that they seldom are the straightforward question and answer exercises most people think they are. Hosts and guests alike usually spend most of their time making assertions, not asking or answering questions.

Our guest today is from the pharmaceutical business, which is under suspicion in many quarters for just about everything from price fixing to bribing public officials. We are told there is some merit in those accusations. Mrs. Brody, you're one of the few women executives in your business. Is this due to discrimination or poor recruitment practices in your industry?

Well, Gene, you must understand that the chemical sciences are relatively new areas for large numbers of women . . .

What the guest overlooked was the provocative introduction, which went on the record, unchallenged. Even though the interviewer dissociated himself from the charge ("we are told"), the interviewee has in essence agreed with it by obediently responding only to the direct question. It's a common mistake, born of tension and the undeserved awe in which guests hold broadcast hosts. Nervously, they wait for the *question* to be posed, suspending their response until they pick up the final statement that ends in that interrogatory tone. These statements, they think, are not worth noting. Very dangerous.

Equally dangerous is not listening to the conversation of other guests. The host may suddenly turn to you for your opinion of another guest's comment, and woe to the guest who is silently rehearsing his or her next answer instead of listening. Actually, the process is the same as dinner table conversation. It's rude to ignore what other people around the table are saying.

It's suicidal on television or radio. Let the rest of the show take care of itself. Concentrate on what's entering the microphones now. And that applies from opening credit to the host's "Thank you very much for coming by."

The ultimate example is a show like the *MacNeil-Lehrer Report,* which originates from two cities (sometimes three simultaneously). The anchor in one city may suddenly look up and ask for a response from a guest in another city, who more often than not looks like a startled rabbit as he responds. Even if participants in the show are a continent apart, they're all on the same show and should listen accordingly.

If *Be yourself* is the first rule, *Be a good listener* is the next most important commandment. All else follows those two.

And if Mrs. Brody had *listened,* she could have defended herself. The host sets the rules, and he changed them by making that assertion. If the interviewer has a right to make assertions before asking the questions, the guest has a right to make—and respond to—assertions before answering. Obviously, if you're going to counter those assertions, you've got to remember what they are. If that sounds impossible because you have not been blessed with total recall, feel free to take notes. Not long verbatim transcripts, but a word or two to refresh your memory when it's your turn. Good interviewers don't hesitate to make notes, and neither should the guest. It looks more professional than trying to kid the public that you have every fact, statistic, and argument in your head. If you do have that talent, by all means go in barehanded. Just be sure you're right. One goof can destroy 30 minutes of triumph.

CHAPTER 19

BASIC TRAINING FOR GUERRILLAS

The problem with dealing publicly with a difficult question is nothing new. Television just makes it a lot more public than it's ever been before.

When Alexander the Great invaded India, he had a group of Indian wise men brought before him. Alexander told the wise men that he had a question for them, and just to make things lively, if they didn't come up with the right answer, they would be put to death.

Question: "Which is the cunningest of beasts?"

Answer: "That which men have not discovered."

Pretty wise, eh?

Alexander thought so, too. He let them off.

Today's spokesmen do not face physical death if they fail to answer difficult questions put to them by the media, but they can do great harm to their careers and their organizations if they don't watch their step.

Twenty years ago the stakes were not so high. The establishment, if not trusted, at least had not lost the respect of the media and the citizenry. A businessman or politician who was on the carpet was treated with a certain amount of courtesy, and his side of the story was given the benefit of the doubt. Questions were not so tough. Answers could be obfuscated without repercussion. But the counter-culture revolution of the 1960s and Watergate of the 1970s changed all that. Establishment critics have learned to use the media as effectively as those in power. Newspaper and television reporters no longer fear to ask incisive, even lethal, questions, and an appearance on TV means ocean-to-ocean coverage.

Ten years ago, not many people had the expertise to deal with a tough media attack. Actually, it didn't even have to be an attack. After one of the early oil spills, *The New York Times* reported that the president of the company that was responsible answered a simple question about the event with a statement that got him into a lot of trouble.

This particular oil spill had done considerable damage to coastal wildlife, which was dying in droves amid the sludge and gook of the spill. When the president was asked about this ecological disaster, his response was: "I am amazed at the publicity over the loss of a few birds." That statement turned the country against him and everything he stood for. He repudiated the statement and the *Times* apologized, but the damage suffered by his company was very great.

Until comparatively recently, spokesman after spokesman, official after official, said things equally damaging to their cause without a second thought. Each time there was a public exchange, a lamb fell. Politicians shuddered over George Romney's assertion that he had been "brainwashed" about Vietnam. When Spiro Agnew said: "When you see one slum, you've seen them all," reaction was even worse.

Something had to be done. And it was. Spokesmen who survived developed an approach that minimized the dangers of public appearances, based on five simple rules:

Be prepared. Even if you are given short notice—or no notice at all—you should have the facts and other information you need at your fingertips.

Have conviction. Express your opinions and explain your cause with enthusiasm. If you aren't excited about it, why should anyone else be?

Be specific. Vague answers suggest that you are hedging or that you can't back up your arguments. Specifics are more convincing.

Be anecdotal. Examples and narratives help to dramatize a point so the audience will remember it. Using anecdotes also makes a response more conversational. It need not be clever, like the Alexander the Great story at the beginning of this chapter, and it need not be profound. It should simply illustrate a point.

Be correct. All the preparation, enthusiasm, specifics, and anecdotes are useless if they're wrong, or if a speaker gets them mixed up or hopes no one will notice the departures from truth.

By following this advice, a speaker has built-in armor for all confrontations, which in turn can save a speaker from a dangerous outbreak of temper. When you are sure of your position and well prepared, it is difficult for an adversary to bait you into losing your temper.

As governor of New York for 15 years, Nelson Rockefeller got all the experience he needed in the art of confrontation:

Student: I'm from the Attica brigade and I'd like to make a concrete proposal, that the stuff that's going on at Stony Brook, where I'm a student, where you floated a bond in order to pay for dormitories being built, where we have to pay off the interest on those bonds which your brother's bank, Chase Manhattan, bought and is reaping the profits off that interest, is the stuff that we poor students have to pay for. I think that's an outrage. You run the state like a corporation. We're interested in taking the billions of dollars that you own and the billions of dollars that you control and dividing it up among the people who deserve it, and not yourself.

What that means is not your slavemaster of a father, throwing dimes to people in the streets. What it means is not a thin veneer of liberalism like the Rockefeller Foundation puts forth. But taking all the money, all the banks, all the factories, all the plantations in South America, and dividing it among the peoples of the world.

Rockefeller: I'd like you to take a good look here, because the only reason this young man is in this room is because I'm Governor. Let me just say this. When I took office as Governor of this state, there were thirty-eight thousand full-time students in the state university. Stony Brook didn't exist. I broke ground at Stony Brook. Only because of this administration are you getting a chance to get a college education, and a good education. I am so glad that we've got a free enterprise system—look at me, will you please. I'm talking to you. You ought to be so glad we've got a free enterprise system where the state can sell bonds and somebody will buy them, so we can build these institutions.*

Conviction and control, in the face of a personal attack.

There are some basic tricks in this trade, many of them adapted from debating techniques. They spring from a ground of common sense, and basically boil down to a single premise: Never let the host or the other panelists control your contribution to the show. Reserve that privilege for yourself.

The first and greatest tool, bridging, gets you from where you are in a conversation to where you would rather be. The best guests don't evade the difficult questions. Only amateurs try that, and most are trampled in the ensuing pursuit. If you evade a question, it will probably be asked again. If you evade again, attention will be focused on your evasiveness, which is exactly what you don't want.

But a good guerrilla knows that it is possible to restructure a question before answering, and in so doing to remove the worst dangers. You do this by volunteering additional information, or different information, beyond that required by the question originally posed.

If it is done skillfully enough, it may be possible not to answer the question at all, without looking evasive. Bridging requires a phrase or clause or

*Recorded live by the author at a press conference.

sentence to move you away from the question to a preferred position. It can be something like, "Let us consider the larger issue here. . . ."

Or, "Before I get to that, let me fill you in. . . ."

Or, "Instead of that, you should ask me about X. Let me tell you what happened. . . ."

The permutations are endless. And the better the fielder, the smoother the transitions. A real pro can use bridging to make sure *his* points are covered in the conversation, regardless of whether he is asked about them. A trained guerrilla volunteers much more than the required information when he or she likes a question. When the question is too delicate, or tangential, or petty, the trained guerrilla volunteers nothing. No question is sacred, and none need be answered slavishly. That's how amateurs get caught. You are entitled to say everything you choose to say about all the topics that are raised, whether the initiative was somebody else's or your own. You do not need to answer specific questions. It is possible through this technique for the interviewee to control the exchange by originating more interesting matters than the interviewer has brought up.

Consider the following by Ralph Nader. Having answered a number of other questions, he bridged to *his* points:

The real questions to ask are, how much do the oil companies need from consumers? If Exxon, for example, as it admitted today in the papers, gave $49 million over a nine-year period to Italian political parties, including the Italian communist party, how much are the oil companies going to demand from the consumer, and get, if they have Washington working for them as an accounts receivable, jiggling the system so as to maximize the price impact on consumers?

Or, is the question how much are the oil companies going to demand to get because they are not competitive? Indiana Standard, for example, is in joint ventures with other oil companies. The idea there is a conspiracy, every day and every week. It doesn't have to be a conspiracy. They are in partnerships, they are in joint ventures in pipelines, in overseas production, in offshore drilling. They have products exchange agreements.

They are all interlocked and that is why they can't really have an arms-length competitive posture, particularly since they are all moving to control more coal, more uranium, and they already control the gas and they are moving into geothermal.*

One could have wished for less verbiage, but Nader definitely controlled the interview. It did not control him.

Bridging can get you out of the most difficult situations:

Daniel Schorr: Mr. Meany, there's an important election coming up in the first district of Ohio this week. If it turned out to be the third recent by-election to be lost by the Republicans, that clearly would have an enormous influence on the others?

George Meany: I don't know. Dan, I don't know what the situation in that district is. *I do know* [here comes the bridge] that in the fifth district of Michigan, which was Jerry Ford's old seat, that this was a strong Republican district. I think Jerry Ford won by forty or fifty thousand votes—I don't know exactly—just fifteen months ago. And that in this district—it was rather a strange campaign—the two candidates, their names

*© *Issues and Answers*. American Broadcasting Companies, Inc., 1975. Reprinted by permission of ABC News.

91

were almost identical, and the issue was brought up by the Democratic candidate. *The issue was President Nixon and his administration. It surely looked like a referendum on the president.* Now more Republicans voted in that special election—I don't know if you got the figures—but more Republicans voted in that special election than did Democrats. Here was a special election where the Republicans have held the seat since 1910—sixty-four years—and where Jerry Ford himself held it for a quarter of a century, and it goes by a fairly substantial margin, to the Democrats. Now this to me *looked like a referendum on the Nixon presidency.**

The amateur would have said he didn't know about the election in Ohio, and he might have stopped right there. Meany implied that Americans everywhere, even in Gerald Ford's congressional district, were of the same opinion that he was about Richard Nixon, "by a fairly substantial margin."

George Meany not only bridged to make his point, but he used another tactic admirably: labeling. Look at the italicized portions in the second half of his answer. The question revolved around Republican fortunes that were failing with the electorate. Schorr asked about a particular race Meany was unfamiliar with. So Meany simply answered the question by bridging to a race he knew and then, because of his preparation and conviction, he was able to leave a very strong impression with the audience that even Republicans were fed up with Nixon. He did it by labeling. Three times he says the issue was Nixon and attaches the label "referendum" to it. His reasons or supporting arguments follow, and then he restates his label.

George Meany was clever and seasoned enough to come up with apt phrases on the spot, but the average guerrilla must think them through ahead. ("Plan your ad libs in advance," said a radio program manager many years ago. Don't worry about the contradition in terms—it is very good advice.) A label shouldn't sound rehearsed, so don't force it. But if you prepare properly, you can always plan a line of attack to work in a label quite naturally. The danger is overworking them. Three mentions is ideal.

A good label is hard to refute and easy to recall. Meany was a master at this (he once called the chairman of the Federal Reserve Board "a national disaster" on *Face the Nation*), but we've had some other public figures who also knew how to profit from labels. One of the greatest labels was "Iron Curtain," popularized by Winston Churchill to describe the isolation and rigid censorship in the Soviet Union and its satellites after World War II. Other good labels that have stuck include Peace Corps, New Deal, Cold War, Great Society, Silent Majority, and "counterculture."

Labeling can be very effective if it comes in the form of a catchy title or phrase that aptly summarizes the speaker's point. Because words fly by so fast on the air, a good speaker makes sure that the point is made more than once, but not belabored.

The third basic tactic is turning the tables and questioning the questioner. Ralph Nader came close in his set of rhetorical questions outlining his feelings about the oil industry. But there are situations that demand an actual question of the interviewer or other panelist by the interviewee: when you need to buy a little time or organize an answer to a particularly difficult question, and when you need a definition of a potentially dangerous word or phrase used in the original question. In any case, you must take the initiative to get to the issue *you* want to raise.

One of the best examples—maybe the best ever—involved Senator Eugene McCarthy on PBS in 1968 during the presidential primaries, in which he was a candidate. Not only does the senator completely de-fang a potentially damaging question from Martin Agronsky, but he does so in very good humor:

Agronsky: Your name is on no major legislation. Why is that?

McCarthy: Well, name me four people whose name is on major legislation. You've been looking at the Congress for twenty years.

Agronsky: Well, uh. . . .

McCarthy: How many pieces of major legislation? Who do you get?

Agronsky: Well, there is. . . .

McCarthy: Well, all right. What was passed in the last Congress? Who put his name on a major bill at the last Congress? Who put his name on a major bill in this Congress? Just one out of 100.

David Broder: Without getting into this. . . .

McCarthy: No. Let's have it.

Broder: You have been in the Congress for twenty years. What do you look back on. . . .

McCarthy: No, let's get into this. You fellows asked this question. Now tell me one name that went on a bill last year.

Broder: I guess it was a bad year. . . . *(Laughter.)*

McCarthy: It was a bad year for major legislation, huh? What about the year before?

Agronsky: Well, one thinks of things like the Fulbright resolution.

McCarthy: All right, Fulbright. But that's because he's chairman. You were going to include the Holley Tariff, Martin, and the Sherman Anti-Trust Act. When was that,1903 or 1897? The Sherman Anti-Trust Act.

Third Interviewer: Senator Kennedy has the reputation as a creative and imaginative legislator. Now. . . .

McCarthy: He has, huh? What did he create or imagine?

Third Interviewer: I'm telling you that's his reputation. Do you feel that is something less than an accurate representation?

McCarthy: *(Ignores the question, wisely.)* I used to have my name on what was called a major bill every year in the House of Representatives. It happened to be listed as a major bill. You know that little journal that comes out that says "Major Legislation Passed"? There was one in there which said, "To Suspend the Imposition of Tariff on Imported Scrap Metal." That was mine. I put it in every year because I knew you fellows and my opponents would always say, "McCarthy has never had his name on a major piece of legislation."

Agronsky: Well, you say that it's insignificant then.

McCarthy: Well, it is. I can tell you things that I have influenced significantly. . . . *(bridge)**

Those are the fundamentals: bridging, labeling, and questioning the questioner. If all humans were born with the same talents, there would be a fourth fundamental: a sense of humor. Humor can be a devastating weapon in the right hands; in the wrong hands it can ruin a cause faster than lying. If humor comes naturally to you, don't shut it off when the little

*Used with permission, WETA-TV.

red light goes on, but if it doesn't come naturally, forget it.

Teddy Kennedy, whose sense of humor is usually good, was essentially humor*less* in 1979 when he faced a question like Agronsky's from Roger Mudd on *CBS Reports.*

Mudd: If you are to be judged as a new and stronger leader, then why is it that the three issues that you're so deeply committed to on Capitol Hill—the national health insurance, closing tax loopholes, and the decontrol of oil prices—have really gotten nowhere?

Kennedy: Well, ah, I think in some of these areas . . . in health . . . that we've made some progress. Some of the areas we've been unable to make progress. If you take, ah, the health insurance proposal, Harry Truman suggested it, Medicare, in 1948. We passed it in 1964 in the United States Senate. It took a good deal of time for the country to understand the nature of that, ah, particular proposal. It takes time.

Mudd: But that's, don't you think that's going to be an issue that'll turn around your campaign, is how effective a leader you were on Capitol Hill? Won't they come at you and say, you haven't had a vote yet on national health insurance, Senator? What kind of leader are you?

Kennedy: Well, the . . .

Mudd: You can't even get it out of subcommittee.

Kennedy: The . . . of course it wasn't even referred to our committee until . . . the national health insurance proposal, even though it has been debated and discussed, for example, the administration's, ah, own proposal was only introduced, ah, within the last, last very few, last very few weeks, after two and a half years of this administration. I don't . . . I had felt that we would have a President that would, ah, stand for that particular proposal. We have had administrations that have opposed national health insurance. Ah, I think without having a President that feels strongly about insuring that we are going to have a health system which is going to, be a decent quality health care at a price people can afford. That we're not going to, we'll have a very, very difficult time in overcoming the power of the various, ah, interest groups.*

If your brand of humor is heavily tinged with sarcasm, be careful. Don't turn it against the host. You may win the battle, but the chances are you will lose the war for the hearts and minds of the audience.

Only the rarest master, like William F. Buckley, can get away with ridiculing or humiliating a guest or opponent. Here he is in a debate with Senator Lowell Weicker of Connecticut at the time of the Watergate hearings:

In the committee room on the 29th of June, here's what he [Weicker] said: "True Republicans do not go ahead and threaten, and God knows Republicans don't view their fellow Americans as enemies to be harassed. I can assure you that this Republican, and those that I serve with, look upon every American as a human being to be loved and wanted."

That was June 29th. On June 30th, a fellow American and a fellow Republican comes to visit Senator Weicker. Charles Colson. Charles Colson as a fellow American and a fellow Republican, yearning to be loved and wanted, seeks to inform Mr. Weicker of his position, and he is greeted with the following words, quote: "You make me sick. Just get your ass out of my office. I don't even want to talk to you anymore."

I would remind Mr. Weicker of Exodus the 23rd, that goes: "If you should see the ass of him that hateth thee lying prostrate underneath his burden, by no means desert him. Help him rather to raise it up."*

If you've got it, use it. If you don't, don't try. It's that simple.

*Firing Line. Used with permission.

CHAPTER 20

FORMS OF SUPPORT

You may be alone there in front of the camera and the microphone, but reinforcements can be all around you. If you want to say something that someone of greater reputation or fame said before you, don't hesitate to call up the memory of that greater person. Plan ahead by placing a couple of quotes on your note cards, or at least the names of the people who said the wise things that support your cause.

Why stand naked on the subject of American military strength, when you can say: "General Gavin, who knows a lot more about this than I do, has said the same thing I'm arguing today. In 1974, he said. . . ."

If your reinforcement is a statistic, make sure it is a clean, easy-to-grasp figure. "A Gallup poll last month showed that 76 percent of the American people also agree with me that. . . ." Beware of complicated statistics: "Some economists have estimated that if the top 10 percent of the individual stock market investors threw their weight behind the same portfolios as the top 3 percent of the institutional investors. . . ." You've lost your audience before you get to the payoff.

Statistics that can be followed on paper can't always be followed by ear, especially when you are comparing barrels of apples and pecks of peaches with quarts of tomato juice. No more than two statistics per utterance, please, and make them the same denomination. You can say a poll showed that 60 percent agreed with you and only 10 percent were dead-set against you. But you can't expect the audience to follow a statistic that says 60 percent of those over 55, half of them city dwellers and a third of them women, are opposed to a 6 percent tax cut if services also are slashed 5 percent.

Statistics are best used for points of comparison, in a set of two. If you are making a point that something has decreased dramatically in recent years, you can say, "Ten years ago there were six million bicycles clogging the state's parks. Today there are only three million." The audience may not remember the exact numbers, but they will remember the significant decrease. If your company has dramatically increased its budget for research on pollution control, you can say, "Five years ago we spent $6,000 on research to stem pollution. Now we spend $715,000 every year on pollution research." People will remember that the statistics showed a significant increase, a decrease, or that things stayed about the same. That's all they really need to remember.

When you cite a statistic or a set of two, keep them separated from other statistics you may need for ammunition later. Cite your statistic cleanly, as if there were a little trumpet flourish on each side as punctuation.

When you can, cite a personal experience to prove your point. ("I was there and I saw for myself.") For instance, in defending the press, refer to your part-time job on a local newspaper while you were in college, and mention that you never heard a reporter ordered to screw all the candidates of a given party. The experience need not be totally analogous to the issues at hand, only similar. It's the "I-saw-it-myself" part that does the trick.

One last warning on statistics: Make sure that the statistics you are quoting mean exactly what they seem to. There are few things worse than quoting the wrong statistics—not missing the numbers by a couple of percentage points, but quoting General Motors when you mean General Electric, or giving the number of farms when you mean the number of farmers.

Look at what happened to former Secretary of Agriculture Earl Butz with Paul Duke on NBC's *Meet the Press:*

Duke: Dr. Butz, more people are leaving the farm today, farm income is down, and the foreclosure rate is up. What are you going to do about these things?

Butz: It is true, Mr. Duke, that people are leaving the farms today, but that is nothing new. During the eight years that Mr. Eisenhower was president and Mr.

Benson was secretary of agriculture, we had a 28 percent reduction in number of farms in the United States. [*Duke, you will note, talked about people leaving farms, not the number of farms, but the hapless secretary forged ahead anyhow.*] Then, during the eight years that Orville Freeman was secretary of agriculture, and we had Democratic presidencies, Mr. Kennedy and Mr. Johnson, we had a 33 percent reduction in numbers of farms. [*He's done it again.*] During the first three years of this administration when Clifford Hardin was Secretary of Agriculture, we have had approximately a 10 percent reduction in numbers of farms. [*And again!*] This doesn't mean that we approve of it. All three of those secretaries did all they could to alleviate the pain of adjustment. They pushed rural development programs, they tried to develop alternative opportunities for those farmers that were leaving the land, and we propose to push rural development just as hard as we can. [*Whoops, now he is talking about people leaving farms.*] On top of that we propose to do everything we can to restore profitability to agriculture and get decent prices and fair income for the family farmers.

Duke: Nonetheless, Dr. Butz, you have said, I believe, that we will have a million fewer farms by 1980. What can you really do to stop this trend?

Butz: Yes, Mr. Duke. When I said we were going to have upwards of a million fewer farmers by 1980, that didn't mean necessarily that I approve of that. I simply was reporting what is going to happen.*

Nothing did Butz any good. When they asked about farmers, he talked about farms. And when they asked about farms. . . .

Meet the Press, December 1975. NBC News. Reproduced with permission.

CHAPTER 21

WHEN YOU'RE ON THE SPOT

It's one thing to know what the fundamentals are, but it's another to use them properly. All the conviction, preparation, and determination you can possibly muster for a given situation will do no good if you suffer an attack of blind panic or—worse—surrender your independence to the host.

The broadcast studio is a foreign land for many talk-show guests, but its similarities to real life are greater than its differences. Just as you may laugh at stories of American tourists abroad who are stunned to discover that there are people who don't speak English or trade in the dollar, you can laugh at the stories of talk-show panelists who forgot they were engaged in a conversation, debate, or argument.

In a conversation, even one that's not particularly argumentative, it's not unusual for one participant to call an opponent's statement into question, to argue context and assumptions, or even to insist that a statement is false. What happens in the broadcast studio is no different. The guests who get into trouble are intimidated by their surrounding, nervous about talking in public, or concerned about ingratiating themselves with the host. This is not the army. The host is not the general, and the guests are not privates. They are equals. It is not only permissible, but frequently necessary, for the guest to challenge the host's statements, and even to refuse to answer a question as stated.

Some people—even lawyers—make the mistake of comparing a one-on-one broadcast interview to a courtroom situation. A broadcast interview is structured, but it does not have legal ground rules. In the courtroom, the witness must answer the questions of the unfriendly lawyer, but if that lawyer goes off base, the witness's counsel will rise to his defense and call foul. He will object to leading, irrelevant, immaterial, and any other kind of question that falls outside what is permissible and reasonable. On the other hand, the friendly lawyer will get up and question our subject in a way that brings out his side of the story. In a broadcast interview, the subject must be his own defense lawyer, and if he doesn't take that role, he's in trouble.

Look at what happened to the president of the American Bar Association when he failed to act as his own counsel. He was asked what the odds were for getting a good lawyer to handle a typical legal problem like divorce or an accident case. The president prefaced his answer and postscripted it, too, but what the audience remembered came right in the middle: "I would say that the odds are about three to one. . . ."

Even if the answer to the reporter's question was knowable, it was not quantifiable, at least not in those terms. The witness stand is not a good model for a broadcast interview, and some questions dare not be answered on their own terms. An alert guest must remember that. For instance:

The guest was a highly placed executive in one of the world's largest oil companies. The interview had been tough but fair for the first four or five minutes. Then the host rolled out a grenade.

Host: I find it peculiar that during the late sixties you people were telling yourselves that a fuel shortage was coming. You were telling the government that a shortage was coming. But you were telling the innocent public to drive more! Buy! Consume! Now, was this irresponsibility due to greed or ineptness?

Tight closeup of Mr. Oil's face. He blanches perceptibly. Was he thinking of an answer at all, or was he planning a particular kind of exile for his company's public relations director who got him in this spot? After about three seconds of awful silence, the nimble reply came:

"I guess it was ineptness, Fred."

That is a perfect example of the "A or B dilemma." It occurs frequently, stemming probably from the human love of simplicity rather than from real malice. In broadcast news, interviewers and editors seek short, no-nonsense answers, sparing audiences long, complicated explanations. They want to keep the show moving at a quick pace. The problem arises when the guest obediently tries to answer an A or B dilemma question exactly as it was posed, even though neither is the best choice.

Such either/or questions are very frequently asked in political debates. A clever, experienced politician slips out easily:

"Tell me, senator, how do you stand on abortion? Are you for it or against it?"

The senator, no fool in these matters, is neither for it nor against it. He is for certain bills and procedures that might satisfy the pro-abortion public and he supports others favored by the anti-abortionists. He refuses to take the bait. Instead, he rattles off in machine-gun style the full range of his opinions. The audience can't exactly follow him, but at least they know he does not wish to appear to be on one side or the other of the question. And the host is mollified by the senator's earnest attempt to state his position without using up too much air time. The senator has not given a simple answer to a complex question. He has shown that he has opinions on the matter.

The A or B dilemma is a favorite game of talk-show hosts and TV newsmen. At its worst, it causes obfuscation of the issues and confuses communication instead of enhancing it: "Is your company more interested in profits or the public?" or "Who is more difficult to deal with, Syria or Libya?"

Even at its best, the A or B dilemma is not an especially throught-provoking way to delve into an issue. Why does it occur so often then? Is it just laziness or ineptitude on the part of the reporter? Neither. Whether a filmed or taped interview is two minutes or two hours long, a reporter or host must come up with excerptible material to justify his or her time. In an interview, the reporter is not going to limit the subject's answers to 20 seconds, even though 20 seconds may be all that is destined for broadcast. Instead, the reporter tries to construct questions that will, by themselves, elicit brief, pithy answers. A news broadcast cannot cover all the ramifications of a subject. TV wants answers that are short and simple. And most times, because so few people are initiated into the mysteries of the broadcast interview, the A or B dilemma question gets short, simple, extractable responses, even when the question is ridiculous.

When the person expected to answer such impossible questions actually tries to do so, the level of the show as a medium of information drops precipitously. Not just because the answer is usually as ridiculous as the question, but because the interviewee has surrendered his autonomy. From there on, the host becomes an authority figure. He has proved he can manipulate. If you, the guest, lose control of a question, you lose control of the interview. If the host had a particular dislike for you or your cause, it's an invitation to squash you. And if the host *likes* you or your cause, he may prefer to keep your statement out of the proceedings, for fear that you will embarrass both yourself and the good people you have come to speak for.

It is folly to let the pressure of the moment force you into a true-or-false, yes-or-no quiz when neither of the choices really serves your purpose or conveys your position.

This does not mean that you refuse to answer all A or B dilemma questions. When the proper answer is A or B, say so:

"Did your company contribute money illegally to the Committee to Re-Elect President Nixon, yes or no?"

"We did not."

You don't want to take two minutes to answer that one, to get it restated, or otherwise play with it. You don't want to bridge to another subject, even if the answer was yes. But in that case, you might take some time to admit the blunder and wallow a bit in expiating your guilt.

CHAPTER 22

THE DUMB QUESTION AND OTHER PERILS

Even the best interviewer can have that off-moment when the head bone is not connected to the tongue, resulting in an unbelievably dumb question. It happened to Harry Reasoner in Rome after the death of Pope Paul when he wondered aloud before a panel of assembled experts why there was a need for a new Pope anyhow.

But more often the unbelievably dumb question comes from an unbelievably unprepared interviewer or an abysmally ignorant one. The sort of person who would ask an energy expert if the Alaskan pipeline was built because the oil would flow downhill from the North Slope without benefit of pumps is beyond help.

As was the ABC newscaster in Chicago, who once spent several minutes with an interviewee discussing "dante" between the United States and the Soviet Union. He forgot to mention the inferno.

The temptation to make fun of the interviewer's ignorance is to be resisted at all cost. Patiently explain that zero base budgeting is different from deficit spending and then go on to make your point. Pronounce détente correctly as you answer the question, without referring to the interviewer's version. You score points for being a nice fellow, and yet you prove that you do know the difference.

The dangerous thing about the dumb questioner and dumb questions is that the door opens for the vindictive guest, another panelist who has been waiting to get you and who now seizes control of the show. Certainly when a guest scores a coup and takes control of the show, the energy level of the exchanges tends to go up, and there are some hosts who delight in relinquishing control to the guests just so some sparks can fly.

This is particularly true of hosts of some panel shows when the subject is controversial and the panel has representatives of every conceivable side. It is much easier and safer for the host to sit back and let the combatants slug it out verbally, questioning each other, directing the discussion toward opponents' weaknesses and fighting to keep it there, or simply hogging the mike and expounding on a favorite topic.

The kaleidoscope of opinion represented on most panels is no accident. The technical broadcasting term for this is covering one's ass. If the show includes representatives from all sides of the issue, no side can accuse the station of being unfair later, even if certain partisans got more play than others. Some hosts will go so far as to pretend to wrest control of the show from time to time with no success. You can tell when that is happening, because the host permits one guest to interrupt another in the middle of an answer, uses a momentary pause to return the panelists to a previous subject that has already created a heated exchange, or actually uses a pause to give another panelist a chance to take control: "Well, Mr. Smith, do you have anything to ask Mr. Jones on that question?" Mr. Smith may not have anything to ask Mr. Jones on *that* question, but he certainly has a grenade he wants to throw into the fray, and his bridge is the easiest in the world. "I think I've heard all I need to hear from Mr. Jones on that question, but I would like to ask him. . . ."

Remember, even if the station or the show or the host operates under minimal rules of fairness and consideration, no such rules apply to other guests on the show. Expect loaded questions from fellow panelists.

Aside from the entertainment value, a show whose host abdicates responsibility to direct and control a panel discussion seldom rises above the disaster level. Only in a one-on-one situation can it be a plus for the interviewer to relinquish control through a dumb question or just plain by accident. At that point the interviewee is in the same enviable position as the President of the United States delivering a television address.

CHAPTER 23

THE LOADED PREFACE

Sometimes in a talk show or interview situation a perfectly good question will go sour. "Given the low regard in which the business community is held, why would anyone getting out of college want to go into banking?" Perfectly good question. But just one little adverb can throw it off: "Given the *deservedly* low regard in which the business community is held, why would anyone getting out of college want to go into banking?"

Suddenly one question has become two issues. If the guest, a local banker, has come on the show to explain the opportunities in his profession, he has a choice. He can focus on the word "deservedly" at the risk of being led into a cul de sac whence he will never return, or he can dismiss the charge and bridge right to his point. The trick is to defuse the insult clearly and to move away from it with a determined manner so that you squelch further probes, by either the interviewer or fellow panelists.

Frequently it is possible to anticipate loaded statements. If so, prepare your defenses. Preparation doesn't just mean getting your side of the story straight. It also means anticipating the arguments of the opposition. If, for example, our banker knew that his opposition was the Socialist Party candidate for mayor, he could have anticipated something like this: "We all know that the business community is the most corrupt group of lawbreakers since the days of Jesse James. How do you have the nerve to ask young people to enter it?" The phrasing changes but the charge is the same, and so is the danger. If the banker is to get to the business he came to conduct, he can't get into a sparring match about Jesse James vs. modern day business.

If there is one question you dread being asked, rest assured that it will be asked. And woe to the man or woman who does not have an answer prepared. In both these cases, the banker could have used a variation on a standard reply. He could have anticipated that some question of business morality would come up, and knowing his host or fellow panelists, he might have anticipated that it would come up as a loaded preface. The banker could acknowledge that some people do feel that business has betrayed the public, although he personally feels that the business community as a whole should not be held accountable for the acts of some, any more than another recognizable group should be branded

113

for the acts of a few of its members. "But because some people do feel negative about the business community, it is even more important to recruit bright, eager young people into the world of business and banking where they can contribute the kind of leadership that business needs in the future. . . ." And suddenly the banker is right where he wants to be.

Walter Wriston, chairman of Citicorp (the First National City Bank of New York) obviously had anticipated the hard questions before he appeared on *Meet the Press* when Lawrence Spivak asked him this question:

Spivak: Mr. Wriston, I would like to ask you something about the banking business. There is a growing number of people who believe that the banking industry exercises just too much power over our economic life. As head of one of the largest and most powerful financial institutions, how do you respond to that charge?

Wriston: You say there is a growing number of people who say that. I frankly have very little evidence that that is the fact. The banking business is the most fragmented major industry in the United States. The largest bank in the country has less than 5 percent market share. I would doubt whether any other industry is so fragmented. Secondly, there are 14,600 banks in the United States serving communities across the country, and the biggest power is exercised where there is no competition, but the facts are that today the relative power of the banks has declined.

I will give you a specific example. The first loan I ever made on airplanes was for a DC-3 that cost $125,000. The legal limit of our bank at that time—we could finance about ten. Today an aircraft costs around $25 million, and a single bank can finance only about four. So, relatively, they have not kept up as fast as they should with the growth in our economy.*

No matter how loaded the question, there is always a way to disarm it, but the interviewee must anticipate that someone will ask it. He can disarm it by disagreeing with the loaded part of the premise, or by acknowledging that some people may feel that way, but then he can proceed to his own point in a swift bridge before his adversaries have a chance to turn the discussion in their direction. But no matter how carefully you review all the possible ways you can be challenged, it is probably impossible to guarantee no surprises. Just be as careful as you can, and then keep on the alert during the show.

All this is good advice for a polite, civilized talk show. But what happens when the opposition is not polite, when they interrupt the answer to a loaded question, and then refuse themselves to be interrupted?

When such an exchange begins, the person who starts the attack, who first loads the question and then interrupts the answer, is usually seen as the villain by the audience at home. Make sure this point is established for the audience. Let the person interrupt you two times before you make a real move. Some panelists will take advantage of your good manners and shout you down every time you start to score a telling point. Let them get away with it exactly twice. Twice is enough to establish the offender as a true boor.

The third time lean forward, smile, and, if you can,

*Meet the Press, April 1975. NBC News. Reproduced with permission.

"You have been characterized, Mr. Stronson, as an ignoramus, a fathead, and a turkey. Would you care to respond to that?"

touch the person and say, "Just a moment please. I wonder if I can just finish this point." Your startling movement should be enough to throw the person off the track so you can ask for the floor. Whatever happens, don't be *as* rude as your tormentor. Smile graciously as you request the floor.

If you are truly outraged, you can throw caution to the wind and let go with an insult, but on the whole, a straightforward unemotional approach is the best.

There are a couple of wicked back-alley techniques to be used on a television show that has commercials. Ask the host how long a given commercial will last, once the commercial break has begun. Then start counting silently. When you figure about 5 seconds are left before going back on the air, turn to the man who has been giving you so much trouble and tell him his fly is open. Then smile. If the troublemaker is a woman, tell her she has lipstick on her teeth. If she isn't wearing lipstick, ask her if she knows she has something caught between her front teeth. And don't forget the smile.

There is a special form of the loaded question used on telephone talk shows, on both radio and television. When the subject under discussion is highly controversial, or when the panelists are political candidates in a particularly close campaign, it is not unusual for various supporters or pressure groups to line up a brigade of troublemakers in front of their phones. Some will ask questions to make your opponent look good, and some will ask questions to make you look bad. If you can be sure that a question you dread will be asked on a regular talk show, you can be positive that it will be asked, restated, and reiterated on a telephone talk show.

CHAPTER 24

THE IRRELEVANT QUESTION

Sometimes your appearance on a broadcast interview is not entirely by choice. You are there because you, or your company, or the group you represent has been a subject of controversy, and now it is time for a spokesman to go on the record about what has happened. The interviewee may not relish this experience at all, and in fact may prefer that the subjects range far and wide, so long as the questioning never focuses on the danger zones. The temptation is strong to pretend that the reason for the visit is far removed from the actual issue, but it is a temptation to be avoided. In the David Frost interviews, former President Nixon did his best to confine the Watergate questioning to one segment—but that's the one program that got a real audience.

The question of what is relevant in an interview is a shared decision between the host and guest. When a host badgers a guest who shies away from difficult areas, he is not being nasty. He or she is merely doing the job at hand. If you agreed to come on the show to discuss the recall of last year's production of widgets, it should come as no surprise when the host gets impatient with your endless recitation of the community services your company has performed. The widget recall, however unpleasant for the interviewee, is the matter at hand, and a fit target for questions, so it is the host's job to steer the interview back on track.

With that exception, there are many times when the host's decision to pursue a dangerous or unpleasant subject is indeed irrelevant. The host represents the legitimate curiosity of the audience, but neither host nor audience can define the full range of what you are prepared and qualified to talk about, and what is simply beyond your expertise.

You must remember that the host's job is to see that the show is stimulating and entertaining, if not exciting. Sometimes an interviewer will proceed along a strange line of questioning to throw you off balance, to produce a provocative quote, or just to see how far an interviewee will go. Maybe you're on one of those shows which throws together a panel of guests without any thought to what they might have in common. Unfortunately, it's not unusual to find a talk show in which the panel consists of an actor, a vegetarian, a former welterweight boxing champion, a balloonist who hopes to cross the Pacific, and a microbiologist. When such a motley bunch starts talking about the impact of a recent Supreme Court decision, a guest who is seriously affected by the discussion can get into trouble. A careless statement can be taken out of context and played on the nightly news, along with its author's affiliation and title.

Here is the horrible, if partially hypothetical, example. On just such a show, with just such a mixed bag of guests, the subject of marijuana comes up. This is a subject everyone has an opinion on, however ill informed. In the midst of this discussion, it is time to introduce yet another face on the show, bidding farewell to the aging matinee idol who must hightail it to his dinner theater performance (all duly plugged by title, location, and length of run).

Host: Our next guest is Mr. Wonderful, President of Youth Services of America. Mr. Wonderful is also a practicing attorney in Duluth. As a lawyer, sir, do you feel that marijuana should be legalized?

Mr. Wonderful: Well, speaking just for myself, I have long felt that marijuana laws are too harsh on young people. We have no evidence that it's even harmful.

Host: Then you do believe that marijuana should be legalized?

Mr. Wonderful: Certainly decriminalized, yes.

Then it is the vegetarian's turn to discuss its herbal properties, and the microbiologist's turn to discuss the dangers of paraquat contamination, and the balloonist's comparison of a marijuana high with the natural high of floating under a bag of hot air. Harmless drivel, right? And before the show is over, each panelist gets a moment to plug his or her special project. Mr. Wonderful, in fact, lives up to his name with an impassioned plea for inner city group leaders, with a beautifully recited anecdote about a gang leader who persuaded his whole gang to join Youth Services, and how this led to college scholarships for many and good jobs for those whose education stopped at high school.

But the next day in the newspapers, and perhaps on television too, the president of Youth Services came off a little differently. "Youth Service Chief Says Marijuana Not a Crime," was the newspaper headline. Which segment of the talk show made the evening news?

You can discuss anything you want to on television, so long as you remember that you are quotable—and not necessarily in context. The newspaper readers and television viewers who didn't see the talk show don't know that Mr. Wonderful was merely participating in a long-running conversation. All they get is his statement. And no amount of "speaking for myself" or "in my opinion" can dissociate the statement from the job title. Remember Betty Ford, speaking for herself about the possibility of her daughter's having an affair? What people remembered, if they disliked her, was the First Lady endorsing premarital sex; if they liked her, they praised her for being realistic.

The danger is particularly great on a talk show that is prerecorded for later broadcast. Often these shows are not shown in the most advantageous time periods, and one way they can entice audiences is with teaser promotion spots. What better come-on than that little snippet of the president of the Youth Services more or less endorsing marijuana? Television is a business, remember, and audiences are customers.

"I find that nothing improves my speeches so much as being quoted out of context!"

What should Mr. Wonderful have done? First, he should have remembered why he was there. He was not invited because he was a Duluth lawyer, a fine fellow, or an original thinker. He was invited because he was president of Youth Services. In that role, he had to remember that certain subjects were off limits, dangerous, and, in fact, subjects about which a person with his title could say little or nothing.

If Mr. Wonderful had a finely tuned sense of humor, he could have laughed at the question and defused it:

(Sincere chuckle). You're asking the president of Youth Services of America whether he thinks *marijuana* should be *legalized?* It's not something that comes up in our business meetings.

Or, if humor did not come naturally:

The members of Youth Services believe in their duty to God and country, and at present the law of the land says that use of marijuana is illegal. I think the members go along with the law of the land. Besides, [he bridges] the people of Youth Services currently have much greater and more immediate issues to work out [and he's off telling the story of how his organization helps troubled kids become good citizens].

It helps in such situations to think of yourself as the personification of your title. What would the public relations director of the Widget Company say to this? What would the First Lady say to this? What would the president of Youth Services say to this? What might be an issue of great interest and firm feeling to you, the person, may *not* be an issue your title should comment on. Before you answer such an irrelevant question, think how it will look attributed to your title tomorrow morning in the newspaper or tonight on the news.

CHAPTER 25

THE ABSENT-PARTY QUESTION

Remember when you were little, your mother told you not to say anything behind someone's back that you wouldn't say to his face? There's a corollary in television. Say anything you like about your opponent's positions, his illogical assumptions, his useless conclusions, his insubstantial arguments. But never question your opponent's motives, his sincerity, or his devotion to the cause, especially when he or she is not present. You weren't the only one who got that lecture from your mother. We all dislike the person who attacks someone who isn't present to defend himself.

Host: Doctor, I agree with you that medicine has the most capable and dedicated professionals in the world.

124

But if that is so, why are people like Ted Kennedy out to get you?

Doctor: I'll tell you why. Because our friend wants to be President of the United States and he doesn't give a damn who he has to step on to get there. He doesn't care about the nation's health. He just wants a hot issue.

The doctor may have found that exchange personally therapeutic, and his friends will all congratulate him on a needle well jabbed. But how does that look to the viewer out there anxious to understand the issue of national health insurance and willing to let this discussion help him form an opinion? Bad, that's how. They see a jerk insulting someone who isn't even present to defend himself. Don't attribute ugly motives to your opponent. It makes the audience question *your* motives, and consequently distrust your position.

Nonetheless, questions about people who aren't present roll on, partly because they are a wonderful device to keep a debate going.

Monday

Interviewer: Mr. Youthful Consumer Advocate has recently said that the labor movement is the single greatest cause of inflation in this country. How do you respond to that?

Aging Labor Leader: Well, this is not the first time that he has commented on things he knows nothing about. He should stick to helping the consumer and stay out of labor economics.

Wednesday

Interviewer: Mr. Aging Labor Leader feels that you are not qualified to speak about matters of inflation and the like. [*Note the casual misquote.*] Is this an area you feel you should stay out of?

Youthful Consumer Advocate: Of course not. I don't know exactly what Mr. Aging Labor Leader meant, but I do know that before his advanced years began to take their toll, there was great mutual respect between the consumer and the labor movement.

The interviewer got a hot debate going at the expense of the two guests. The Consumer Advocate, in particular, made the mistake of accepting the paraphrase as being what the Labor Leader said. It sounded like an insult, so he slung one back. If a quote is out of context, and you're not familiar with it, there is no reason to accept its veracity. There are all kinds of ways to sidestep such situations. You can make a mitigating remark ("I find it hard to believe that he said this, but if he did, I certainly can't agree with it, because . . ."), or you can simply address the issue and ignore the personal aspersions. Or you can take the hard line: Defer the answer until you have seen the exact quote, context and all, for yourself.

It's amusing to read both exchanges together, but there is no guarantee that the audience for Monday's show is the same as the audience for Wednesday's show. Even if it were, how many would remember—as they watched on Wednesday— exactly what was said on Monday? You can't assume that the audience knows anything more than you are providing at the moment they see the show.

Of course, it's possible that an absent person did really say something as bad as it sounds, so you don't want your response to sound like an evasion. Just don't be baited into making a remark you'll regret.

CHAPTER 26

THE WHAT-IF GAME

During any talk show of reasonable length, inevitably the host will invite one or more of the guests to play a game of "let's pretend." If one or more of the guests are politicians, it will be sooner rather than later, because the press and the politicians just love to play the game of who will run for office. A typical exchange begins: "I know you haven't announced your candidacy for governor as yet, but what if Governor Incumbent makes good on his threat not to run for re-election?"

Even the greenest politico has learned to reply: "Well, the governor has yet to make any announcement about his plans, so it is premature for me to

127

speculate on what I might or might not do." Then, if the guest has been doing his homework, he will bridge deftly to a topic he prefers, as follows: "Really, George, I don't think the audience cares about idle speculation on my possible future at this point, particularly when they have just had a taste of the new 7 percent sales tax. You know that I have been deeply involved in the effort to streamline our state tax structure, in an effort to reduce the burden of the individual taxpayer. . . ."

Politicians have been trained to sniff a hypothetical question a mile away, but other talk-show participants, lamentably, can be seduced into playing the game. The trick is to develop that same sense of danger when the questioning turns from the straightforward to the conditional, and decline to play the game. If you don't decline, well, here is an excruciating example of what can happen. Fortunately, our Mr. Oil's answer wasn't on the air. Here is the question:

Mr. Oil, in *The Crash of '79*, a novel, Paul Erdman presents a very convincing scenario for nuclear war in the Middle East. Considering the recent revolution in Iran and Mr. Erdman's rather startling predictions about the area, do you think if the United States were faced with an anti-American coup in Saudi Arabia that something similar might happen? This is not to suggest that yours or any other oil company would be part of any such plan, but if the situation were to explode in Saudi Arabia as it did in Iran, do you think the United States might just go in and secure those oilfields before something happened to them? I'm, of course, not suggesting in any way that you would have anything to do with an actual U.S. invasion of Saudi Arabia, but you do think it could happen?

Forget the disclaimers. Forget all the mitigating phrases that seem to take the burden off the oilman. Even though Mr. Oil himself thanked the reporter for his care in phrasing the question, he went right ahead and answered it by outlining a detailed plan of attack on Saudi Arabia to make its oilfields safe for American consumers. By the time he got through, nobody in the audience remembered the disclaimer, only this horrifying, detailed plan to invade someone else's country.

Had he done this in front of a camera on a regularly scheduled show, the nightly news would have had a winner to lead off with that night. Save "what if" games for your children and grandchildren.

CHAPTER 27

THE INCONSISTENCY TRAP

It can happen, without warning, to any guest on any show. Suddenly the interviewer says, "In 1970, you were saying such-and-such. Now you are saying something sharply contradictory. Why is that?"

If the question is entirely unexpected, it can throw a guest over the edge of panic. His or her face flushes, perhaps even visibly through the pancake. The pulse races, that awful metallic taste rises on the back of the tongue, and the front of the tongue starts tripping over lame excuses. "Well, look . . . it really isn't all that, uh, contradictory. What happened was that . . . well, this happened, and then that, you know, and, in the light of whereas, wherefore, whereby, and whereif, you can see how this is at the present time."

The guest has fallen into the trap. He has been accused of being inconsistent, or worse, opportunistic, and his reaction has done nothing to allay the suspicions suddenly raised in the minds of the audience.

Who said your views have been irrevocably transcribed into an official record after the first public utterance? When faced with a charge of inconsistency, admit it. You are allowed to change your mind. In fact, it shows growth and flexibility. And if you once felt that way but no longer do, just say so. "Yes, it is true I felt that way then. But I have changed my mind." Or, "When I said that, I had not had a firsthand opportunity to investigate the situation for "I was brainwashed," putting an instant end to his made a difference in my opinion."

It is not a sin to change your mind for good reasons. It is also not a good idea to change your mind on serious subjects too often. If you do, people will think you aren't serious about your statements— you will be accused of being wishywashy and undependable. One 180-degree turn per serious issue per lifetime is the limit.

The sum total of a person's opinions on the issues of his time is what makes a person identifiable. Thus, if you are forced to change your mind about an important issue, don't try to toss it off. Take the time to explain why your opinion was modified. The worst thing you can do in a broadcast situation is to leave the audience with the impression that your old view still prevails. If they agree with your old view, they will be very upset to find out later that you no longer hold that view, and if they disagree with your old position, it is important for you to make it perfectly clear that you have come around to their way of thinking.

Only a favored few can get away with cockiness—a beloved character, a certified curmudgeon, perhaps, who can say, "Oh well, I used to lie a lot." It may work for them, but unless you're one of them, don't try it out in public for any serious issue.

For some reason, people who can be perfectly frank about many embarrassing topics have a hard time admitting, "I've changed my mind." They find it even harder to say, "I was wrong."

In 1948 South Carolina's Strom Thurmond ran for President of the United States on the "Dixiecrat" ticket. During his campaign, he said, "There aren't enough troops in the army to force southern people to admit Negroes into our theaters, swimming pools, and homes." In 1978, Thurmond made a speech to the Senate in favor of the bill to make the District of Columbia a state. That new state's two senators and one representative would, no doubt, be black. Thurmond said, "I think it's the fair thing to do." A smart-aleck commentator could have concluded that Thurmond favored the admittance of more blacks to the U. S. Congress, but not to swimming pools and theaters in South Carolina.

When you do change your mind about some important issue on which you have taken a strong stand in the past, you should say so publicly and without equivocation. Whether it's a simple matter of new evidence, or a radical change of heart, you must say so. If you don't, you'll bite your tongue talking out of both sides of your mouth.

Double-talk has broader reaches than personal opinion. The National Cancer Institute joined a researcher at the University of California at Berkeley to allege that a particular ingredient in hair dyes was a carcinogen. The agent is 2,4-diaminoanisole, 2-4

132

DAA for short. The Food and Drug Administration agreed, and proposed a health-warning label like those on products containing saccharin and on cigarettes, stating that 2-4 DAA had been shown to cause cancer in laboratory animals.

The people in the hair-dye industry were thrown into a turmoil. Spokesmen from the companies and the trade association launched into a blitz of television and radio appearances to deny emphatically that 2-4 DAA was dangerous to people's health unless a person *drank* 25 bottles of hair dye every day for something like 75 years. Most of the spokesmen were staff chemists, who insisted over and over again, "Our products are *perfectly safe*."

Meanwhile, between television appearances, these same chemists were reformulating the hair dyes to replace the 2-4 DAA with another agent. Their actions seemed to be a direct contradiction to their public statements. Although the hair dyes have been reformulated, the appearance of an inconsistency remained. Eventually, the companies explained that they undertook the reformulation only to avoid the warning label, whose presence might unduly alarm consumers. The public still wonders about their true motives, and inconsistency remains in some people's minds, even though the hair dyes are "still perfectly safe."

One of the most famous pratfalls was taken by George Romney, who, in his race for the GOP presidential nomination in 1968, became dovish on the war in Vietnam, in contrast with his early hawkish stance. One night he went on the late Lou Gordon's talk show in Detroit, where Gordon observed: "Governor, you used to be a hawk on Vietnam, but now you're a dove. What happened?" Romney answered,

133

"I was brainwashed," putting an instant end to his career in national politics. Americans apparently will stand for a lot from their presidential candidates, but brainwashing?

Romney's unfortunate assessment of his change of heart prompted Eugene McCarthy, who wanted the job himself, to comment, "George Romney was brainwashed! A light rinse would have been sufficient."

Romney should have taken the question seriously: "You know, Mr. Gordon, I wasn't satisfied with my position on Vietnam. I wasn't sure I was right. So let me tell you what I did about it. I went over there for a couple of weeks on an inspection tour—at my own expense, incidentally. In that time I tromped around and had conversations with a lot of people who really know what's going on. Then I thought about it all, and you know what, Mr. Gordon? I changed my mind."

The flip retort is an option available only to the antic few, whose position in the public's affection is already secured.

CHAPTER 28

"NO COMMENT"

Those two words should never be heard from a guest on a television interview. But sometimes there is no alternative. Interviewees who find themselves in that position can help themselves immeasurably by coupling those two words with an explanation for the response. Saying *why* there is no comment can take the sting out of the refusal to answer.

Don't say "no comment" when you mean something else, and don't say "I don't know" when you mean no comment. "No comment" is not a substitute for "I don't know." A person who says he doesn't know the answer to a question when in fact he doesn't, comes off as honest and aboveboard, and this in turn endows him with vulnerability and all those other warm qualities that endear an interviewee to the folks at home. *But:* saying "I don't know" too often makes the interviewee look like a dunce.

Charles Bates ran the FBI office in San Francisco all through the search for the kidnapped Patty Hearst. It was not a good era for the reputation of the FBI as an effective law enforcement agency, but Bates rescued what he could from the affair by remaining constantly available to the press. When someone would ask about the state of the Patty Hearst case, he'd get up in front of the microphones and answer quite truthfully in his Texas drawl: "Ah have to tell ya, we haven't any AHdea wheh that girl is." He didn't know, and he said so.

It takes a special kind of talent to do what Robert Strauss did in an exchange with Edward P. Morgan on *Issues and Answers* when Strauss was chairman of the Democratic National Committee. In essence, Strauss said "no comment" to two questions in a row, but watch how he did it:

Morgan: If a Democratic presidential candidate asks your guidance as chairman of the party as to what would help to rebuild the Democratic party further in terms of policy toward Southeast Asia, what would you say at this juncture?

Strauss: Ed, I'm not going to start, I can think of no worse disservice I can do this nation than for me to start rebuilding American foreign policy vis-à-vis Southeast Asia or anywhere else. That's not my background. I have no expertise there. It would be demagogic, it would be purely partisan politics. It wouldn't do anyone any good. There is no point in my answering a question like that. If they want to know what they can do to help rebuild the party to capture the White House, I would be glad to give them some advice on that subject.

Morgan: What might propel Ted Kennedy into the nomination is a deadlock which would shift the action from the floor (of the convention) to smoke-filled rooms. Do you see the possibility of a deadlock with Mr. Wallace on one side and Mr. McGovern's supporters on the other?

Strauss: In the first place I'm going to eliminate from the question the Wallace and McGovern names. In the second place, I'm going to eliminate from the question the "smoke-filled rooms." I'm going to rephrase the question to suit myself and then I'll answer it.

Morgan: Okay, go ahead.

Strauss: I think there is a very good chance that we will have a multi-balloted convention. I think anytime you have a multi-balloted convention, you're obviously going to have negotiations between various constituency groups, as to candidates to suit them, trying to build a ticket that, number one, satisfies the delegates, and number two, you can win with. And I think it's far too early to tell what the possibilities—what the odds are on that, but it's a real possibility that that will take place, and I think that when that does, there are any number of people that our party could turn to. I can think of a dozen people, no one of which I will name right now, that could head our ticket and head it well and give us a candidate with character, and with courage, and with perception of the needs of this country.*

By bridging, by rephrasing the questions, and by sheer verbal pyrotechnics, Robert Strauss said "no comment" twice, and got away with it. No one

---

*© *Issues and Answers,* American Broadcasting Companies, Inc., 1975. Reprinted by permission of ABC News.

listening casually would even be aware that he never answered either question, and actually refused to answer them quite frankly.

What's more, Strauss managed to turn those questions around in such a way that he said exactly what he came on the show to say. Not only did he avoid the trap inherent in the questions that might polarize his party, he managed to turn it into a commercial for the glories of the open, talent-heavy Democratic party.

Senator Edward Kennedy has a tendency to compound his no-comments whenever he is asked a question about Chappaquiddick. Here's how he did it in an interview with Roger Mudd on CBS in 1973.

Mudd: From your political assessment, Senator, of 1976, would you say that Chappaquiddick remains the largest single obstacle to your getting the nomination?

Kennedy: Well, I don't know what the considerations would be for anyone seeking the nomination in 1976. I imagine issues have the ability to separate candidates. They did in the primaries, and have as long as I've been active in national political life. And so I expect they would be. How people are going to make their mind up, of course, is something else again.

Mudd: But you spoke a minute ago of desire for an inspirational leader who will invoke public trust and confidence. At the same time, public opinion polls indicate that—I think one out of three do not trust you, and it all stems back from Chappaquiddick. That's the reason for the question. Will that in itself, given the climate of '76, in your judgment, prevent you from getting the nomination?

Kennedy: Well, as I say, that's going to be something that would be decided by the people, and I'd hope that were I to be a candidate and go to the people in the various primaries, they will make a judgment on

it. It's going to be up to the people to make a decision
on it. And I believe that they will make whatever
decision they will at that time.

Mudd: But don't you have any feeling as to which
way they will judge you?

Kennedy: Well, I don't. I mean, I think they are
going to have to make a . . . as I say, they are the ones
that make the judgment. That's a decision for them to
make. All I can do is present myself, my views, respond
to any of the questions that they might have, present
what I think are the principal issues before the country
in 1976, be compared to any other candidates that may
be a candidate in 1976, and let the people decide.*

Kennedy does do one good thing in this exchange. He never utters the word Chappaquiddick.
This made it difficult, if not impossible, for one of his
answers to be taken out of context and quoted as a
news item. Each one of his evasive answers stands
alone and speaks to the election, not the subject
raised by Roger Mudd. He may look slippery to those
who are watching this interview, but he has saved
himself further embarrassment by providing no ammunition for a news clip.

By 1979, Kennedy had apparently decided that
he couldn't explain his actions at Chappaquiddick
because he didn't understand them himself. Coin-
cidentally it was Mudd again who did the interview for
CBS Reports:

Mudd: *(Preface)* Kennedy himself is probably recon-
ciled to having Chappaquiddick with him always. But
no matter which questions are asked of him, he still

does not seem at ease with the answers. And he still talks about Chappaquiddick in a rather bloodless, third-person way, referring to his own conduct that night, for instance, as "the conduct." Do you think, Senator, that anybody really will ever fully believe your explanation of. . . .

Kennedy: Well, there's, . . . the problem is, from that night, ah, I found the . . . the conduct and behavior almost, ah, sort of beyond belief myself. I mean, that's why it's been . . . but I think that's, ah, that's the way it was. That's, that, that happens to be the way it was. Now, ah, I find it, as I've stated, I found that the conduct in, in that evening . . . as a result of the impact of the accident, and the sense of loss, the sense of hope, and the, the sense of tragedy, and the whole set of circumstances, that the behavior was inexplicable. So I find that those, ah, those types of questions as they apply to that . . . questions of my own, ah, soul as well. But that happens to be the way it was.

Mudd: The American voter is left with three choices. One, that Kennedy's account of a tragic accident is believable, and is therefore of no political consequence. Two, that Kennedy's account is not believable. But that knowing any other account could have ruined a career which since Chappaquiddick has become substantial, makes it an acceptable defect. Three, that Kennedy's account not only is a fabrication, but is also a major flaw that disqualifies him from the presidency.*

John Gardner, then head of Common Cause, knew exactly how to say "no comment" in May of 1973:

Herman: Mr. Gardner, Common Cause has mobilized its members to press Congress on many pieces of legislation in the past. Have you now begun any studies or staff work on what position Common Cause should take, should Congress move to impeach President Nixon?

Gardner: No, we have not, and we certainly feel that as long as the present investigations are in progress, no citizen should have a closed mind on that subject.

Herman: Mr. Gardner, I'd have to say that your first answer was clear and precise, that you have not begun any studies. But is an impeachment of a President of the United States the kind of thing which you think Common Cause should take some role in? Should it happen, will you act and put pressure on Congress for what you believe in one way or the other?

Gardner: I think that this is far too serious a matter to speculate on while the evidence is still being reviewed, while several investigations are still in progress. It's a very grave step, and I think it would be wrong for us to comment on it or to speculate on it at this time.*

Gardner didn't answer the question, but he did say why he wouldn't answer, and that makes all the difference.

CHAPTER 29

HAPPY ENDINGS

Except maybe for his mother, nobody cares who is the associate producer for *Firing Line.* If the audience at home hasn't vacated altogether for bathroom calls or sandwiches while the credits crawl across the screen, the chances are it's *you* they're watching, not the names and titles.

Don't slump in your chair and stare blankly into infinity waiting for the signal to go home. You'll look like a penitent serf who has just been flogged for misbehavior. The show is not over until you are out of the building. Instead, lean forward. Smile pleasantly. Engage the host in a continuing conversation, the way the guests often do on the *Tonight Show.* See if you can get the host to smile, even if it isn't Johnny Carson.

Gesture as you chat (not obscenely, please). Even if you have been taken through the wringer, your body language will tell the people at home that you may be beaten, but you are not cowed. You will fight another day. And if the experience was pleasant, it's all the more important that you show how pleasant it was. Otherwise the viewers at home may think your true nature is something other than that charming, intelligent, witty spokesperson they have just met. Sometimes it's the only weapon you have left after the encounter, especially if you have just been William F. Buckley's guest.

What do you get for your trouble? Well, because of the *host's* smile and general affability, the audience may come to the conclusion that you're not such a boob after all. That's better than nothing.

At best, somebody at home might get the idea that you had a lot more to say on the subject than the show permitted you to reveal. Think about it. There you were, caught in a heated exchange, or without that one statistic that would have clinched your argument. You may have made a horrendous mistake, but that's all it was, a mistake. And you prove it by bouncing back, the TV equivalent of jumping over the net or shaking hands at the end of a title bout. You're down, but you are willing to set a rematch. You have style.

The best part about it is the way *you* take the initiative in this maneuver. It was *you* who leaned forward to make a point while your opponent was plastered to the back of his chair in rapt attention. It was *you* who gestured, while the formerly hostile host smiled and nodded in response. With this as the last impression made by the guest and host on the audience at home—just visually, of course—who is the victor and who is the vanquished?

At the very least (and this is almost below the acceptable minimum), you won't look as if you can't wait to get the hell out of there.

Almost always, 99 percent of the time, the microphones will be off at this point in the show. The credits usually roll over theme music or a sound effect and a phethora of promotional announcements about the show next week, what's on tomorrow night, or who's playing whom on Saturday.

But are those microphones really off?

Just as you don't count on dead microphones before a show, you don't trust them afterward, either. Fortunes have been made by the collectors of "bloopers" committed by innocent people on radio and television who thought those microphones were off. If you assume that you are on the air until you are back in your car, you won't become instantly famous for reasons other than you intended. If you permit yourself, just once, after a particularly disagreeable interview, to lean forward in your chair and call the host a "son of a bitch," cheerful smile notwithstanding, you can be sure that's the time the engineer was sound asleep at the switch.

ADVANCED GUERRILLA TACTICS

All good advice can be taken too literally, including the basic training course in this book. Because the fear of public appearance is so strong in most people, we have attempted to equate a TV appearance with some more common and restful social occasions, such as a dinner party or a conversation in a friend's living room. Such comparisons are good in that they help counteract the tendency to blind panic, but they aren't entirely apt.

In regular social conversation, politeness dictates that one follows the lead of one's partner in conversation. And on such occasions people speak in a fashion that usually has a kind of sequential development. For example, a neighbor may tell you an anecdote about his child, the upshot of which is a trip to the police station to bail the kid out of trouble. At the end of his story, he may turn to you and ask if you ever had the same problem with your kid. The response desired from you is clear. If you have such a story to tell, answer the question by following with your own anecdote. If not, you make a philosophical observation on why your child is so well behaved. You are not expected to comment on the details of your neighbor's dilemma. In fact, if you were to dwell heavily on the details of his dilemma, probably you would be verging on the rude.

Quite the opposite is true in a television interview. Your worst response in such a situation may be to answer the direct question at the end of the interviewer's anecdote or assertion. Your best response may be to make a point that seemingly had nothing to do with the question asked, but which defuses, clarifies, or amplifies an earlier part of the statement.

Here you *begin* your response with the most important point you wish to make on the subject, instead of building up to it as a conclusion, as you might in normal conversation. Thus, if you are interrupted, cut off by time, or otherwise prevented from finishing your normally leisurely response to a difficult question, your major point will be made. In a social situation, such a response may be seen as overweening egotism.

In a social situation you would not repeat your major themes or points as you must to be effective on television. If you sat around a dinner table repeating the same argument two or three times you would come across as a bore. But in a broadcast situation, you must repeat points if you want the audience at home to remember them and to perceive which of your arguments are the most important.

You are serving an educational function, too, and just as your elementary school teachers would tell you what you were about to learn, give you the lesson, and tell you what you had just learned, a good broadcast appearance should include that repetition of major points.

Refusing to answer a question as posed in a social situation is a sign of discourtesy, either on the part of the questioner who has trod on too personal an area, or on the part of the respondent who has decided to snub the questioner. Refusal to answer a direct question in a television interview, however, is a necessary skill.

American Bar Association President Chesterfield Smith was too polite in answering a reporter's question about the odds of finding a good lawyer:

Reporter: Chief Justice Burger has complained at various times about the incompetence which can be found in the legal profession. What are the odds of ending up with a good lawyer for a middle class American who is faced with a typical legal problem like divorce or an accident case?

Smith: There are lawyers in America who don't have the skills that I would like them to have. It's very difficult to identify them; it's very difficult to select the proper lawyer. I would say that the odds are about three to one that you'll get a very good lawyer if you don't work at it. But if you work at it, the odds are almost 100 percent that you can get a good lawyer.*

*Meet the Press, May 26, 1974, NBC News. Reproduced with permission.

Like any polite person, Smith answered the question in the order in which is was posed, answered it directly, and saved his most positive statement for last. If he had reversed his answer, ignored the challenge to state the odds, and offered a remedy for those lawyers whose skills are lacking, he would have had an effective answer for television. In an ideal response, Smith would have followed his 100 percent odds with some concrete suggestions on how a typical American should go about choosing a lawyer.

Panelists and interviewees who go on a show *to be interviewed* are in grave danger, because they place themselves in a passive role. If they go on to *participate in an exchange of ideas,* they will be much less likely to be hurt by the experience. In this sense, a television interview can be more, rather than less, like a social conversation.

When a guest takes the initiative, the host is sometimes thrown into a passive position. Bridging to new subjects, challenging statements, or asking your own questions forces the host to shift focus to the subjects the interviewee raises.

Although it may be advisable to take control of a program, or to use rudeness in a way you would not in normal conversation, there is a line that must not be crossed. Never be *as* rude or *as* interruptive as the other guy.

An advanced guerrilla, one who is comfortable enough on television to alter his or her natural behavior to fit the situation, must learn some physical self-discipline that goes beyond resisting nervous habits. In ordinary conversation, one frequently nods at the other person who has the floor as he or she discourses at length. The nods have varying meanings—"I agree with you," "I understand what you're saying," "You're right." The nods are a polite, nonspecific way to indicate that you are following what the other person is saying.

But in a television interview, when that long speech may be the tricky preface to a loaded question, nodding can be very dangerous. Imagine that the camera has a close-up shot of the guest, while the host is speaking off camera. The guest is a vice president of a large oil company, and he punctuates each of the host's statements with one of those polite, noncommital conversational nods.

Host: Our guest is a vice president of one of those companies that sat down with the Arabs not too long ago and bartered away our independence; (nod) one of the companies that continues to rape the environment; (nod) that manages consistently to put its company profits before the good of the people. (nod) Now, sir, what are your company's policies concerning minority hiring?

Even if the guest's nods were confirming his private suspicions that this was exactly the form of attack the host would take, or his nods were mental checkmarks reviewing his defense against each of those assertions, how would that look as a snippet on the evening news? Traitor (nod), polluter (nod), opportunist (nod). Even if the snippet went on to show the skillful answer to that loaded statement and question, the impression left with the viewer at home is one of agreement with the charges.

Learn not to nod politely in public. When you are on television, nod *only* when you are in wholehearted agreement with what is being said.

The determined guerrilla takes physical discipline even further. You can't stop yourself from perspiring if your glands decide otherwise, but you can stop yourself from letting that physical lapse work against you.

When Jerry McAfee, chief executive officer of Gulf, was called to testify in Washington before a house subcommittee investigating the "uranium cartel," he found himself perspiring under the hot lights set up for the press and television cameras. During his testimony he reached into his pocket for a handkerchief, which he touched to his brow. At that moment every camera in the press gallery clicked, and all over the country the next day people saw McAfee with kerchief at brow. The implication was not that he was hot, but that he was sweating because he was guilty.

Ideally, you should discipline yourself not to perspire. Practically, if you need to wipe your brow, do it with a forefinger, and discreetly wipe your forefinger with your handkerchief. The finger, if photographed, will make you look thoughtful.

Finally, there is the problem of the reversal. At the conclusion of an interview that has been filmed for later broadcast, the crew may set up some reversals, or reverses. In a one-camera situation, the camera is on you for the interview. To allow editing and provide some variety in the finished product, they will need some shots of the interviewer—nodding, reacting, asking question. So they "reverse" the camera and the interviewer repeats the questions. Frequently, the atmosphere in the final result is a great deal different from what it was in the actual interview. Daniel Schorr explains it very well in his autobiography, *Clearing the Air.*

At lunch in the spring of 1962, [CBS Chairman William S.] Paley complimented me on the recently aired *CBS Reports* documentary on East Germany, "Land Beyond the Wall." Its dramatic climax showed Walter Ulbricht, the East German Communist leader, upbraiding me for my questions and finally storming out of the room in full view of the camera. "What I admired most," said Paley, "was the coolness with which you sat there and looked at him while he was yelling at you."

Breaking into laughter, I said, "Surely you understand that the shots of me looking cool were 'reverses,' filmed after Ulbricht had left the room!" No, Paley had not understood that, and had not known about "reverses" and he wanted all this explained. Feeling as though I was betraying some company secret—albeit to the head of the company—I proceeded to explain in detail the conventional postinterview procedure for shifting the camera and focusing it on the correspondent to repeat the principal questions, plus a gamut of absorbed and skeptical poses, all of this to be spliced into the interview to add variety and facilitate editing. Paley was fascinated.

"But isn't it basically dishonest?" he asked finally. "Aren't you in a position to sharpen your question the second time around? And can't you arrange your reactions the way you would have liked to have them?"

"Absolutely! And that temptation will be there unless you're willing to go to the expense of having two cameras each time." With a sense of plunging deeper, I went on:

"The deception goes much further than that. Let's talk about your friend, General Eisenhower. He recently filmed a series of interviews with Walter Cronkite. I happened to see how a transcript was being edited. At one point, Eisenhower was made to appear to be answering a question he had actually been asked several pages earlier. The producer explained to me that

Ike was sometimes so diffuse that questions had to be rearranged to match his replies."

Paley looked deeply shocked. By the time I was back in Bonn that evening, I heard reverberations from New York. Paley had ordered the summary abolition of subsequently filmed reactions and questions, and any editing that attached answers to the wrong questions. His sweeping order, which had film editors wringing their hands, was later quietly eased to permit "reverses" when approved by the interview subject.*

If a crew asks to do reverses, it is wise to allow them, but don't leave the room. Listen and watch carefully. If the questions seem to have changed tone, or if a change in wording seems to change the thrust of a question, object immediately, while the camera is running. If you don't object on the spot, it will be too late, and subsequent protests will sound like sour grapes. Why allow them at all? The editor needs them for transitions and sometimes to add pace to the interview. Without reverses, you can bet your appearance will be truncated. Of course, if you are making an unwilling appearance, refuse permission. It will do wonders to shorten your time on the air.

*From *Clearing the Air,* by Daniel Schorr. Copyright © 1977 by Daniel Schorr. Reprinted by permission of Houghton Mifflin Company.

CHAPTER 31

USING THE CAMERA

If you find yourself appearing with some regularity in front of television cameras, you will become more comfortable and even begin to use the cameras as professionals do.

In a one-on-one interview (one host, one guest) usually there are three cameras set up to record the action. When properly placed, their positions follow the pattern of an asymmetrical five-pointed star: the host is one point, the guest is a point adjacent to the host; the camera at the point adjacent to the guest is focused at the host, the camera adjacent to that takes in both people, and the camera at the point adjacent to the host is focused on the guest. The guest's

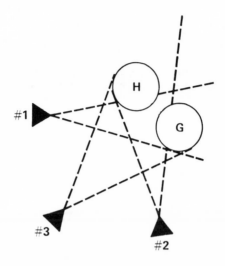

camera is straight ahead of him, over the host's shoulder.

"Properly placed" is an important distinction, because very often the production staffs at television stations put the cameras in the wrong places, which contradicts some of the advice on where to look. But if the guest is seated and can see a camera across the host's shoulder, he or she can figure that is the guest camera.

The guest camera can get a shot wide enough to include the host in the foreground in about a three-quarter profile, but its main target is the guest. And it varies its focus among three basic shots: a "waist shot" (either from the waist up, if standing, or from the lap up, if seated); a "medium close-up," from the sternum up; and an "extreme close-up," the face from the forehead to the chin. The camera does not move as the operator changes focus from waist

shot to close-up; the focus of the zoom lens changes.
In the early days of television, cameras dollied and
trucked to vary their shots, but with modern equipment they move much less frequently. The host
camera is just the opposite. It can get a three-quarter
profile of the guest and the same three shots of the
host.

In some very small stations, this is the limit of the
equipment used, but most stations these days use a
three-camera setup. The third camera provides a
"cover shot," which shows the entire set to the
audience at home, and permits "cutaway" shots.
Switching from one camera to another in a two-
camera setup can get pretty boring over 30 minutes,
so camera three is there to add variety.

If the show you have chosen (or the show that has
chosen you) is a panel show, camera placement may
be somewhat different. It *should* follow the same
basic pattern as the one-on-one, but it varies more
often than not. If you are a single subject in front of a
panel of interviewers, your camera will be just to the
right or left of the panel and behind or beside it. The
panel's camera(s) are behind you and to the side.
Look at the camera, if it catches your eye. Do not
swing broadly from one camera to the far panelist or
vice versa, or you will seem to be playing to the
camera. Simply look at the panelists in turn, although
you may want to wander back to your camera for a
telling point.

Sometimes these shows are set up with the
reporter-panelists sitting in a staggered line or
semicircle beside each other, in a variation of the
one-on-one show, so the "host" camera can see the
entire panel or one panelist at will. Sometimes host
and guest panelists are in a straight line, and a single

camera serves two or more panelists, as if they were one. If you are all sitting in a line, you can assume the cameras will be set up basically in the five-pointed-star position, dividing the participants neatly among them. If you can see a camera off the host's shoulder, you'll know for sure. When in doubt, look at the host and/or your fellow panelists.

In news interviews that are arranged with very little or no preparation, there is only one camera, which should shoot over the interviewer's shoulder at you, the subject. If it doesn't, as all too often happens, the camera ends up getting no more than a three-quarter profile of you and the person with the microphone. This setup has its advantages for a crew with little time, since both you and the interviewer are in the shot and there is no need to film the interviewer separately later, or with another camera.

Where does the guest look if he is going to use the cameras to advantage? Most of the time he looks at the other person or persons on the show. That will always look good to the audience at home. The guest who looks at the host or fellow panelists comes across as "attentive," "respectful," or "involved"—all good qualitites.

But there is even more to be gained by eye contact with the real audience. Think of the camera as one single person in your audience. You might be speaking to millions, but you must never think of those vast numbers. Otherwise you will begin speaking as if you are before a microphone in Madison Square Garden. Your gestures will become the broad sweeps of a public orator, your voice will take on formal cadences, and you will become a caricature. The person you are speaking to is right where that camera sits behind the host's shoulder. If you intend

to make the most of this experience, you must maintain eye contact with that camera, if at all possible, when you are making important points.

You can't always do this, because the director may have cued in another camera at that particular moment, but if you can see the red light glowing on the guest camera as you are about to make your big point, shift a steady gaze to that camera. You shouldn't stare constantly at the camera when the red light is on, however. To do so is to "play to the camera," a self-serving technique that paints you as a phony.

You look at the camera only when and as you would look at a person standing on that spot whose good opinion you desire.

But what if the guest camera's red light goes off, just as you turn a firm gaze toward it? What if it isn't on at all, as you turn to it to underscore the point you are about to make? Have you made a fool of yourself? Happily, no, if the cameras are in the right places. Cameras 2 and 3 by virtue of their placement will make it seem that you are looking at the host, since only your eyes, not your body, are shifting focus. Under no circumstances should you let your gaze wander from the host to the camera and then to the empty air. You will come across to the audience at home as shifty.

You can survive and prosper as a television guest without paying any attention whatsoever to the cameras, but you can add to your effectiveness if you learn how to use them.

The floor director generally stands out of your view, between cameras 2 and 3, where the host can see him or her easily. If by some chance the director should move suddenly into your peripheral vision and you are startled enough to glance at him momentarily, don't let it pass. Your eyes will have shot off for no reason apparent to the audience, and if you don't correct the impression, people will attribute your dismay to what you have just said, or what you are about to say, or what the host has just said. Make a point of explaining: "I'm sorry, Harry. I was distracted for a second by your floor director over there. Let me start again." On the other hand, if you know the floor director is hovering there between cameras 2 and 3, his sudden appearance will be much less likely to distract you.

CHAPTER 32

STYLE
OVER SUBSTANCE

Style, unfortunately, is still more important than substance in television. Short of a videocassette recorder, there is no way for a viewer to stop a discussion while he or she reasons through an argument, so in the end, a viewer's reaction to the participants in a discussion is emotional, not intellectual.

With books, magazines, and newspapers, *what* is said usually is more important than *how* it is said. The *what* makes the news. On television or radio, just the opposite is true. In radio the absence of visual distraction permits a listener to concentrate on content, but on television the sight of a participant who is confused or angry—or groping for words or perspiring heavily—supersedes any statement, and the total impression of the personality is what's left.

The emotional content of the program will remain in viewers' memories far longer than any ideas expressed. If you are very lucky, a viewer might remember one point you make on an interview show. And even after that has faded from memory, the personal impression remains. The viewer will re-member whether or not you are likable; that's all. And that is why losing your temper or lowering yourself to the level of a rude host or a swinish fellow panelist is the worst of all sins.

There is a spectrum of likability. You may be likable because you came well prepared and backed up your statements with crisp, specific examples or well-researched statistics. You may be likable be-cause you showed great humor in the face of adversity, even though you failed to score any of the points you came to make. You may be likable because you became an underdog at the mercy of a bullying host. You can fail at all the objectives in the show and still win, so long as the viewer at home feels admiration or sympathy for you.

Your attitude can work against you too. If you look bored by the questions, if you are arrogant in refusing to defend or explain your position clearly, if you imply that the program didn't warrant preparation, or if you appear to relish the humiliation of a fellow guest whose position you do not countenance, you will lose everything you hoped to gain. You may actually be in the right about certain points, but your style has defeated you.

Likability in some respects has replaced all other

measures for the effective use of television. The Q rating system, which ranks performers by their likability quotient, explains why a number of television performers have been given the chance to fail more than once in a series. If the performer does well in the Q ratings, he or she will be paraded out in series after series until the right vehicle can be found.

Corporate image advertising on television is another example of the power of likability. You can be mad as hell about the prices at your gas pump, but it's hard to blame the supplier when you have warm feelings about an oil company's efforts to reduce pollution, or when its efforts in medical research have brought admirable results.

If your name or face conjures up warm feelings of friendliness in a viewer, you are doing your job on television, even if you have nothing to say and can't make a point on a pencil with an electric sharpener.

Likability, of course, can work against you if you have to share the camera with a star. Television hosts with high Q ratings like Johnny Carson or Phil Donahue, or newsmen like Dan Rather, are among the most formidable of opponents when a difference of opinion arises on a show. No matter how likable you may be, you cannot compete in a single appearance with the long relationship and trust built up between these high-powered personalities and their audiences. If you find yourself on a show with one of them and the going gets rough, only the aptness of your position and the nimbleness of your defense can save you.

If style is more important than substance, then it holds that the style of a well-liked host is infinitely superior to the style of a one-shot wonder. Total preparation and total conviction are your best—and

only—weapons when such an encounter turns sour.
That isn't likely to happen, for the high Q performers
seldom play the heavy, but if it should, be sure you
are not the cause. Minimize the damage by bridging
to a safer subject as soon as the host's hackles show
the slightest sign of rising.

CHAPTER 33

60 MINUTES
CAN BE A LIFETIME

Throughout this book we have been concentrating on a particular kind of television and radio broadcast, one that is live or prerecorded without editing for later broadcast.

Local and national news shows have a wrinkle we have occasionally alluded to: the ability to extract a small segment from a larger show or interview by editing. The editing process is very dangerous, because the subject has no control over whether, which, or how many of his or her remarks will be plucked out for a news show. An interview subject's only defense is to have control over what is said, minimizing the opportunity for an editor to trim the interview into a gaffe.

Ordinarily the staff for a local or network news show has no inclination, too little time, and too much film or tape to edit to worry about skewering someone. The sheer speed at which they work day after day to produce a half-hour or hour news show on deadline is protection enough for an interview subject who has been reasonably careful about his or her utterances on camera. Editors do their best not to make an interviewee sound addlebrained, but in haste an editor may occasionally garble a subject's comment or observation. That happens less often than you might think.

Not everything *you* hoped would be broadcast will indeed make the air. Despite your best efforts, the news staff may not see the news in your comments the same way you do. In fact, sometimes they pick up on one of your incidental remarks, which they see as more newsworthy than what you emphasized. It's their job and their privilege. Next time you'll figure out a way to do it better.

In an ordinary 30-minute news show, there are about 22 minutes of actual news. An average story takes about 90 seconds, and the actualities—the comments from a person interviewed within that segment—generally get about 20 seconds at most. Even at the sprightliest of clips, the maximum number of words an interviewee can expect to get on the air is 85. What can you get across to a dispassionate audience in 85 words—or less? Enough, if you're prepared. Start with the most important 85 words, and then, if you're not interrupted, embellish, restate, give as many examples and anecdotes and statistics as they're willing to record. You'll be safe if you assume that only those first 85 words will make it.

DOONESBURY

by Garry Trudeau

Most of the time the portion of your statement or answer that comes immediately after the reporter's introduction or question is the part that gets on the air, another reason to make your point first and save the details for later. You may think your cause is too complex to state in 85 words, and indeed, with all its facets, it may be. But you must pick the single most important part of your message and deliver that first if you hope to get it across.

Television does not care about the *matter,* it cares about the *manner.* The editor who readies your interview for the air is processing material in a hurry. Yours is not the only tape or film he or she has to worry about. The editor's inclination is to take the question and as much of the answer as he needs for his 20-second clip. If your best-laid point is there in the beginning, the editor will take that, and, in fact, perhaps throw away the rest of the interview sight unseen and word unheard.

After all, within this 22 minutes, the editor may have fifteen or eighteen stories to consider, which shows you exactly how much depth there is to any topic in television news. Walter Cronkite calls TV news a headline service, as apt a description as any. Over the years, viewers have learned to perceive it the same way, and those who seek to use television can't use it well until they understand what TV news is and what audiences use TV news for.

The New York Times prints a complete transcript of the President's press conferences. If you want to know what he said and make your own judgments about it, you must read the transcript. Except for the occasions on which the entire conference is carried live—often in daytime hours when most viewers are otherwise occupied—you will see only clips, what the news editors consider the high spots.

The same holds true for you. When you are on

television, especially in a news interview, the audience never sees you in all your individuality. Unless you are absolutely enthralling, you will never get a chance to explain this or refine that. TV is by nature superficial. If you start with that premise, you can use it very adroitly. Remember: a news show has 15 stories, an interview lasts 20 seconds. Make life easy for the editor by putting your best point forward at the beginning of the interview.

The editing process greatly diminishes the chances of getting your message across as you want it. Most major television stations these days have a documentary unit which produces local documentaries of a generally innocuous nature: character studies of apple carvers or stained glass craftsmen, architectural poems, sympathetic profiles of local celebrities or institutions. More and more of them, however, are also developing investigative news teams to produce prerecorded, pre-edited, investigative series to hype local news ratings. The popularity of the "mini-doc" has grown in direct proportion to the ratings for *60 Minutes,* the first news and information show to reach a par in the audience's affections with sitcoms, football games, and the rest of the mix that makes the top of the Nielsen rating list.

By and large, unless you are involved in a breast-enlarger scam, a bid-fixing gig, or some genuinely corrupt pursuit, the mini-doc crews will treat you with kid gloves. The problem is that news shows, and even public service programs, are themselves subject to rating pressures. The success of *60 Minutes* in the ratings exerts an influence that goes far beyond that particular show. It has spawned imitative magazine news shows on other networks, but even more important, it has made the news directors of local stations all around the country reexamine local news operations with an eye to increasing ratings by adopting as many as possible of the elements that make *60 Minutes* a success.

One of those elements is controversy. More and more, local news operations are encouraging their mini-doc crews to concentrate on more serious and more controversial subjects. (Television still has a way to go to catch up with the kind of controversy that attracts the print media, but tone poems are steadily losing ground to consumer-oriented subjects and such serious social subjects as drug use among teenagers, divorce, and alcoholism.) The moment a mini-doc crew approaches a subject that is not event oriented, the amount of film or tape exposed expands, the number of people interviewed grows, and the amount of editing from raw footage into finished product jumps exponentially. Where once a single interview might have sufficed, four or five arrive for the editor to cut. Each extra interview increases the chances of a strong, telling, controversial piece of material on the air.

If you watch these mini-docs with any regularity, you will notice that they seem more intense, on a higher emotional pitch, than the standard news stories around them in a regular news broadcast. The larger the amount of raw material, the higher the emotional impact after editing can be, with the highest level going to shows like *60 Minutes,* which pursues stories through thousands of feet of film and tape, edited down to the best 20 minutes. And at that end of the spectrum, another issue emerges from the editing process.

60 Minutes has put the entire journalism world in an uproar over the issue of entrapment. This is an issue that extends across the spectrum of the press, both print and broadcast. In 1979 the Chicago *Sun-Times* lost a surefire Pulitzer Prize for its series uncovering corrupt bribe-taking city inspectors in Chicago. The newspaper opened a bar called The Mirage, where cameramen and reporters recorded the visits of inspectors as the bar went about obtaining the various licenses necessary to do business. The Pulitzer jury decided this was entrapment, a technique it intended to discourage by withholding the prize from the *Sun-Times.*

How far newsmen and women can go in gathering stories is a debate that reaches the Supreme Court with regularity. In 1979, *60 Minutes,* which pursues its subjects very aggressively, lost a court fight over the profile of Colonel Herbert and his attempts to alert the authorities to the My Lai massacre in Vietnam. The Court decided that the show was out to get Herbert and therefore skewed the information it uncovered to make him look bad. In journalism, this is known as the "state of mind" decision—it questions the journalist's state of mind at the commencement of his or her investigation into the story.

Frankly, most journalists start looking into a story because they smell a rat somewhere. The rat may not be the person they are interviewing, but someone on whom the interviewee has the goods. The difficulty for someone invited to be interviewed for a show like *60 Minutes* is in figuring out which rat the producers are after.

If they have decided *you* are the rat, you have a problem. Unlike other shows, where stalling an interview can sometimes make a producer lose interest, *60 Minutes* pursues stories for a year and more if necessary. The show will use every resource available, from disgruntled employees to college students who apply for jobs and report what they see, to get the rat they're looking for. Their raw material—background information, film, interviews—goes through a winnowing process that selects only the most telling moments. The show, which makes effective use of reverses (where the interviewer records questions after the interview to be edited in for visual variety), can be the Waterloo of a television guerrilla.

But it can also be the Mecca. When *60 Minutes* profiles someone, it will spend hours, days, and weeks to make that person look as colorful, witty, and interesting as possible. And when it decides to expose someone or something, it uses every vehicle at its command to achieve the objective. Mike Wallace, in particular, is adept at intimidation, and his stories are usually the strongest investigative pieces in the weekly mix. A person without extensive broadcast experience stands little chance in a Wallace interview. He will bully, cajole, play what-if, pose the A and B dilemma, set all the traps and play all the games available to a pro in order to elicit the information he wants from a subject. His kind of success is sharply limited when he is dealing with someone experienced in the media, as H. R. Haldeman proved.

It makes for exciting television, but is it fair?

Some would say no; others would say all's fair in pursuit of information in the public interest. Both sides beg the basic question. Why aren't more people trained to survive such an encounter? The impact of *60 Minutes* on local programming is just in its infancy. Out there are dozens more Mike Wallaces waiting to make a mark, looking for their big opportunity. And hundreds of victims waiting for an invitation to the slaughter.

It isn't enough to train only one person in a company or organization to deal with a television encounter. Crews for *60 Minutes* will proceed from the top person down through the ranks until they find an amateur to their liking. Other broadcasters will learn to do the same. Investigative print reporters have used that technique for years. There are print reporters who think it's just fine if the public is confused about when and how remarks and state-ments can be reported, about the exact meanings of the phrases "off the record" or "not for attribution" and when those phrases can be invoked. It makes their job easier.

It's much harder when a subject says he wants to prepare for an interview first, or when the subject knows that anything he says can be used and attributed to him unless, right off the bat, before any information is exchanged, the reporter agrees that the remarks are off the record (not to be used) or not for attribution (to be used without the subject's name, as in "a high-ranking White House official said today. . .").

In the long run, this knowledge never prevents a good reporter from getting the story. It simply protects the subject from undue grief over a delicate issue. Even the best broadcast guerrillas cannot indefinitely cover up wrongdoing. But if you're not a scoundrel or an idiot, knowing how to handle an encounter with the press will keep you from sounding like one.

You can delay a journalist in the pursuit of a story, you can make sure you put your side of the story forward, but you cannot avoid the encounter permanently without permanent damage to yourself, your cause, or your organization. And so, when the producer from *60 Minutes* calls, check your closet for new skeletons, take a TeleCounsel course (hang the cost), and prepare yourself for the most telling examination of your life. You can pray that Harry Reasoner shows up instead of Mike Wallace, because the show may simply be interested in your warm personality, but if it's Wallace, make sure you've learned how to fight a guerrilla war.

Even if *60 Minutes* itself never expresses interest in you, the fallout from that show's influence on television news in general can still come to haunt you. The local mini-doc crew may do 10 minutes with you instead of the 5 minutes of yore. They may interview your partner, your colleagues, even your enemies. And then the editor will take the best 5 minutes of the lot. Those 5 minutes can be just as crucial as the 20 minutes of a *60 Minutes* segment. At the very least, they will stand out as the emotional high point of the local news show the night they are broadcast.

CHAPTER 34

A SCHOOL FOR GUERRILLAS

"An airline company spokesman said today . . ." is still a common phrase in the nation's newspapers. But such spokesmen appearing before television cameras is a rapidly diminishing phenomenon. With Minicam crews dispatched at a moment's notice, able to operate under the most difficult conditions and to broadcast live from the scene of a news event, something has changed in American institutional life. The spokesman, often operating under strict orders or in ignorance of certain facts, has lost much of his credibility in front of the camera.

The audience expects, and broadcasters have learned to demand, that the spokesman give way to the person truly in charge, whether it is the president of the company or the governor of the state. And institutions themselves are beginning to come around to the idea that the person in charge is the only reliable spokesman in a state of crisis.

The trouble with this is that most chief executive officers of companies or administrative heads of government got where they are for a lot of reasons that have nothing to do with the ability to communicate effectively through the broadcast media. Politicians were the first to pick up on the need for a good television presence, but people in business and government are beginning to follow.

Early efforts by chief executive officers to stand up for their own companies on television can charitably be described as disastrous, simply because so many of them were novices. Here were all these companies with trained broadcast spokesmen who simply could not go on television on behalf of their institutions, while those who *had* to go on knew nothing about the procedure. That's why the Tele-Counsel course began: to train the uninitiated to use the media, to prevent them from being used by the media. Why couldn't things go on as they had? Here's a grim example.

At one Texas oil refinery, no piece of information was permitted to reach the press until it had been discussed, approved, and released by the Management Committee, which met every morning at 10. One evening the manager of the refinery left his office at 5 P.M. to attend a cocktail party and dinner. He neglected to inform his secretary, and was therefore incommunicado for several hours, a highly unusual state of affairs for the manager of a refinery worth hundreds of millions of dollars.

The manager and his wife returned home just in time for the evening news on television. The lead story, live by Minicam from the refinery, showed the place in flames. In the background were explosions and towers of flame hundreds of feet high. In front of the camera, with the conflagration as a backdrop, stood the public relations aide for the refinery. He was surrounded by reporters and had a bouquet of microphones in his face.

"What started the fire?" screamed a reporter over the din.

"What fire?" yelled the PR aide.

Next morning at the 10 A.M. meeting, the Management Committee made an appropriate declaration about the fire and issued a release to the press.

Intermediaries don't always slow the flow of news the way that PR fellow did, but any removal from the source of authority is to be avoided these days.

A typical two-day TeleCounsel seminar takes place in a professional videotape studio. The instructors are professional newsmen, journalism educators, and professional broadcasters who operate as a panel questioning seminar participants in turn, as part of a mock news show. Everything is recorded.

Within the "show" Murphy's Law prevails. The panelists do their best to make sure that whatever can go wrong for the guest does. Guests are prodded until they squirm, insulted until they lose their temper, baited into making foolish statements. It is a grueling object lesson.

The "show," titled *Character Probe,* gets as nasty toward the guests as the instructors' imaginations permit. (Afterward participants are advised never to go on shows called *Character Probe.* Instead, they are advised to look for shows called *The Rotary Club Salutes.*)

Participants sweat through a replay of their first encounter with the cameras, and the instructors conduct a day-long course in guerrilla television tactics. The final exam is another "show" where participants have a chance to practice their new skills.

The panelist-instructors are out to get the guest, and frequently they succeed all too well. During one session the president of a large manufacturing company was asked, "Don't you agree that your company's diversification program in recent years has been monumentally stupid?" He took issue with the word "monumentally," and said that he didn't agree at all. For the next few minutes the panelists led him through a long list of modifiers until he finally settled on "moderately," as in "moderately stupid." The president rejected "colossally," "enormously," "prodigiously," and "unprecedentedly," among others. With each new word, the panel had a chance to relate yet another blunder or example of stupidity on the company's part. The aspects of the diversification program that had been attacked as "monumentally stupid" were "the real estate swindle" and the "record club hustle." He was so preoccupied with finding a substitute for "monumentally" that he never even heard those phrases.

The senior vice president from another manufacturing firm had worked there more than thirty years before he took the TeleCounsel course. During his inquisition before the panel, one panelist muckraked up the charge that the company founder was a raging anti-Semite and had, in fact, bought a newspaper to spread his virulent hatred of Jews. "Have you no conscience, sir, that you would accept money from a bigot?" He dodged the question, but not artfully. "Okay, but how do you account for these expressions of hatred and vitriol against a whole people from within an organization which is otherwise so progressive and ecumenical and decent?"

"Damn it," he said finally in desperation. "There's a bad apple in every barrel!"

Stories like these amuse us, but they are painful to the victims in the extreme. Fortunately, they never happened before a real broadcast camera.

It may occur to you to wonder how you might fare in such a situation where the titans of the business world, who hold so much power over thousands of workers and billions of dollars, did so badly. You would probably do very well, better than they did, simply because you are used to dealing with adversity in personal encounters. In many big businesses, especially at the top, the people around the top executives build protective cocoons around their leaders. They screen out all but the most important visitors and problems and make life as easy as possible for the chief executive. These people are not used to being challenged, especially when that challenge is aimed at their authority or power. They are used to people who carry out their bidding, and that is why, when they first encounter television, so many of them come off so badly.

CHAPTER 35

PROFESSIONAL AUDIENCES

If reading through this book has convinced you to run the other way every time you see a television camera approaching, you can still do your part to make the broadcast game two-sided. Every sport needs its fans as well as its players.

A professional fan who understands the fine points of the game and its rules can actually improve the quality of the performance. Once you are familiar with some of the traditional plays of broadcasting, the game itself begins to look different. Even the Sunday morning news and information shows—*Face the Nation, Meet the Press, Issues and Answers*—take on a new fascination. It is there that over the course of a season you will see examples of nearly every good and bad technique on the part of panelists and guests. Some of the questioners dote on loading their opening remarks. A show seldom passes without a round of what-if or an absent party question volley. It becomes easy to sort out the guests who know what the game is about from the guests who dig themselves a hole and pull it in after them. The shows are leisurely enough to help a spectator spot every play, so it's a good idea to begin with them.

Once you have mastered these, you'll find it easy to apply what you have learned to the faster paced nightly newscasts, where the rankest amateurs appear. With practice you'll be able to tell when a story has been heavily chopped up, and when an interview has been sliced into one sensational quote. A knowledgeable viewer who can spot the tricks of the trade soon becomes skeptical about the accuracy and completeness of the information that does come through, and loses interest in certain kinds of shows, particularly those run by uninformed hosts who permit garrulous guests to take over. The dumb question begins to stand out as if amplified. The evasive answer no longer has the power to deceive. In short, you have become a professional member of the audience, able in numbers—by the switch of a channel selector or the "off" button—to improve the quality of broadcast communication.

The pros don't watch television or react the way an average audience does. If you ever have an opportunity to watch a network news broadcast with a group of local broadcast newspeople, you'll see a really professional audience at work. Instead of reacting to what is contained in the broadcast, they speculate on why one piece was given so much

"If he sneaks in any of his innuendoes, Edward, flip him over."

prominence, and how another piece of film or tape made the show on such late notice, and they will comment on the anchor's show of emotion at a particular point.

They will be discussing the style of the show, rather than its content, because they know that style determines a show's ultimate impact. How someone on a show reacts to a question is far more important to them than what he said. Did he fall for the carefully laid trap or didn't he? Who scored the most points, the interviewer or the subject? *This* important story never made the news because it couldn't be visualized. *That* person, who knows the most about the subject, will not be interviewed because he is terrified of television and refuses all invitations to appear. Television—the medium that gives most people most of their information about almost everything—presents a world that is at best less than the whole story, at worst grossly distorted.

Knowing that this gulf exists between the screen and reality is helpful, but it's not enough. Consuming the news and information product of television without question is downright dangerous. But by knowing something of the television encounter and how it works, a spectator can avoid drawing the wrong conclusions more often than not. Eventually it may lead him or her to question the rules of the game more closely. A broadcast need not engineer confrontation to make a subject interesting. Conversely, television need not be dull to be accurate and fair. It needs only to make the odds even for everyone.

Whether that is accomplished through a massive guerrilla training program or by a change in the medium itself is a question to be resolved by broadcasters and their audiences, aided by informed guerrillas who accept the challenge of the medium and win battles as well as lose them.

The first step in this process may be bad for the broadcast media, because it increases the skepticism of the audience. But it will be good in the long run, because television, like other big businesses, suffers from what its customers (the audience) *don't* know far more than from what they *do* know. It suffers more from what they don't see on the screen than from what they do.

Pollster Burns Roper had some interesting observations on the process of communications in America in a 1975 speech to the Public Relations Society:

As a nation, we have become surfeited with formal communications systems and messages. Nobody could possibly keep up with all the messages conveyed through our elaborate and extensive media complex. I think there is no question but what this profusion of formal communications has increased people's awareness of issues, problems, and abuses that years ago they were oblivious to. While I think this communications system has caused people to be more knowledgeable than they used to be, I think it has also had the unfortunate effect of causing people to *feel* more knowledgeable than, in fact, they are. It would be my further contention that, as formal communications messages have been substituted for face-to-face or one-to-one communication, believability of the messages that have been transmitted and received has declined. . . .

When people can relate to an individual, they tend to pay more attention, and they tend to find what he says more believable than what an amorphous, abstract corporation or other "entity" says. This is not to say that they will fully agree with the individual, but it is to say that they will both listen and have respect for what they hear. . . .

There has developed a "them" complex. You will hear people say, "All television repairmen are a bunch of crooks." Usually, if you ask, "Is your TV repairman a crook?" people will tell you that he is not. "He" is an individual; "they" are a foreign group. . . .

I think it is important that an organization or institution defend itself. One might say with low credibility on the one hand and self-serving statements on the other, it is futile to defend one's self. However, I would say that if *you* don't defend yourself, almost certainly no one else will. Moreover, a non-defense becomes a tacit admission of guilt. . . . Because of the problem of low credibility as well as for reasons of simple honesty, I would "reveal the warts" and "tell it

like it is". . . . To admit one's error tends to take all the
steam out of potentially hostile opponents and, in the
process, to impart a credibility to the individual or
organization making the statement. . . . [I would]
also tell the story to the people who don't know it rather
than to each other.*

Roper was arguing for more openness of communication between big business and the public, but
his advice is sound for anyone who has a message to
deliver. He does not say which medium this individual
should speak through or how these confessions of
guilt should be made, but television would seem one
of the obvious answers.

With television's ability to bring a viewer face to
face with the President, or the head of General
Motors, or a convicted murderer on the way to prison,
we know and experience more than we used to. But it
only seems that way. Like the shadows on the wall in
Plato's cave, the real story is still some distance
away. The directions on how to get there should be
somewhat clearer than they were before this book.

*Reprinted with permission.

CHAPTER 36

A CHECKLIST

If you have a television appearance coming up, review this checklist:

1. Are you familiar with the show you're appearing on—its host, its format, and what is expected of you?

2. Have you rehearsed all possible questions and your answers with someone else?

3. Can you explain clearly in about 85 words or less the major point you need to get across?

4. Is your delivery anecdotal and conversational, or pontifical and argumentative?

5. Have you prepared notes for your own reference?

6. Have you supported your assertions with evidence?

7. Are you going on the show "to be interviewed"? If so, adjust your attitude. You are going on the show *to participate* in a conversation, and you have the same rights on television and radio as in any other conversation at home or in the office.

8. Who is your audience? It is the *people at home,* not the host of the show or your opponents across the table.

9. Can you remember to *listen* before you talk and to challenge the premise on which a question is based, if necessary?

10. Do you have a few bridges or transitional statements in mind? These are lead-ins to the point you have come to communicate.

11. Are you ready to answer any question without resorting to "No comment"?

12. Are you prepared to *restate* your major point? To get it in twice (or more) is good. But make it sound different to the audience.

13. Remember what happens to the muscles in the face when you're nervous? They tighten. Also, under hot lights you may be inclined to hood your eyes with your brows. It will look like a frown to the people at home. Don't do it! Be mindful of the expression on your face. Remember to smile when it's appropriate.

14. Are you prepared to deal with a request for reverses after the interview?

. . .If so, you are in control and ready for television.